WHAT DO WOMEN WANT?

Also by Susie Orbach and Luise Eichenbaum

OUTSIDE IN, INSIDE OUT

and by Susie Orbach

FAT IS A FEMINIST ISSUE
FAT IS A FEMINIST ISSUE II

WHAT DO WOMEN WANT?

Susie Orbach
and
Luise Eichenbaum

Michael Joseph
London

First published in Great Britain by Michael Joseph Ltd
44 Bedford Square, London WC1
1983

ISBN 0 7181 2236 4

Typeset by Alacrity Phototypesetters
Banwell Castle, Weston-super-Mare
Printed and bound in Great Britain
by Billing & Sons, Worcester

This book is dedicated to Jeremy Pikser
and Joseph Schwartz

CONTENTS

Introduction

We opened the doors of The Women's Therapy Centre in London on 8 April 1976 offering psychotherapy and counselling services to women and their families. This was the first project of its kind and scope in Great Britain and we were soon to be overwhelmed by the uptake of our facilities by women from all over the country. Women talked about the emotional upsets that pervaded their lives — about their marriages, about being single, difficulties they experienced in their jobs, the texture of parenting, the meshing of role expectations and changing opportunities for women. In the last six years thousands and thousands of women, young, middle-aged and old, have come to the Centre and shared with us what was on their minds and in their hearts. As the Centre grew we travelled around the country and met women from Leeds, Brighton, Birmingham, Manchester, Canterbury, Southampton, Sheffield, Portsmouth and many more towns throughout England and Scotland. There was great interest both from mental health institutions and women's studies programmes and women's groups about the work of The Women's Therapy Centre. The existence of the Centre helped to remove the stigma for women who wanted professional help in addressing complicated psychological and social issues.

In women's therapy groups and theme-centred workshops women learnt to value their own experiences and to rethink aspects of their lives and their emotional yearnings. Barriers that existed between women from different class backgrounds, different lifestyles, different occupational groups, ages, and even sexual orientations, dissolved as

women discovered together the commonality of their
emotional and psychological experiences. Underneath the
seemingly vast differences in how each individual woman
lived her life were themes, directions, conflicts and anxieties
shared by other women in the group. Hearing them in each
other, women could identify what was troubling them and
get support and encouragement for the changes they
wanted to make.

In revealing themselves and their concerns, the women
who attended the Centre shaped its growth and direction.
Programmes we developed as therapists were propelled by
the desires and the anguish we discerned in the lives of the
women we were meeting. At the very heart of many
women's concerns and confusions was the theme of dependency. In order to understand more about this theme we
thought about our own experience, we thought about the
experiences of our clients in long-term individual therapy,
we examined how this issue came up in groups, we looked at
what happened in couples and friendships and we began to
design workshops that focused on the theme directly.

From the early days of the women's liberation movement
links began to be made between women's economic and
emotional lives. Women in our world were brought up to be
economically dependent on men. We all knew of the
bargain to be made in marriage — women would look after
the house, home and children; the men would make sure
the bills and expenses were met. Many women stayed in
unsatisfactory marriages because there were few alternatives. Even today many women and men who prefer to
live separately continue together because economic conditions are structured with so few and increasingly dwind-
ling alternatives. One of the first issues the women's
liberation movement took up was that of women's second-
class economic status. Many women have become self-
supporting but the battle has yet to be won. Women still
earn much less than men in the same occupational sphere,
women are still the last to get hired and the first to
get fired. The economic structure does indeed relate to

the emotional one but not in an easy mechanistic way.

Many women we encountered had achieved economic independence and they used this independence to reduce their reliance on men. They still sought close relationships but did not allow themselves to feel emotionally dependent in these relationships. A new notion circulated, especially in the women's movement. Relationships in which women felt vulnerable because they were emotionally dependent came to be judged as old-fashioned, not very feminist, too caught up with ideas of romance and ownership of the other and so on. Women were eager to denounce their dependent parts and experience the relief of not being overwhelmed by the cloying intensity and the drama that was so often part and parcel of an intimate relationship. Many women felt freed by not being in close relationships and not fretting, worrying — feeling insecure so much of the time. Women began to see how, often, intimate relationships produced dreadful feelings of insecurity rather than the harmony and sanctuary that close contact with another had seemed to hold out at first. Women sought to be economically independent so that their emotional relationships could take on a different shape.

Our work both at The Women's Therapy Centre and in New York led us to see that the solution to women's 'problems' with dependency was not all that simple. It wasn't that women who could now support themselves were successfully negotiating relationships that didn't stir up terrific longings for contact, emotional inter-dependence and nurturance. Women, whether self-supporting or not, disclosed continuing confusion about the topic of emotional dependency, which pointed out that the relationship between the economic and the psychological sphere was more complicated than might have first appeared.

That is, women involved in relationships with men found that, although they had made enormous changes, their men had not. Women's developing autonomy clearly forced certain issues out into the open for couples. Men were making behavioural adjustments to women's demands but changes in couple relationships clearly required more than men doing the dishes and helping out with the kids. The psychological terrain of the relationships between women and men had not yet been mapped out. In effect men were being excluded as well as let off the hook from making deep personal and political changes.

For us the women's movement had offered another strand. It meant the growth of the emotional side of relationships and not its constriction. Emotional relationships were valued. We relied on friends and lovers and we recognized that dependency. We began to sense that dependency was a problem for both men and women. We didn't want to be in retreat from dependency and knew how very important friendships and love relationships were in our lives. We saw how these relationships could give us support for growth and autonomous development.

We were eager to understand how to look at the yearnings that women felt rather than to reject them and we asked ourselves how men 'managed' their dependency needs. As psychotherapists we knew that attitudes we hold are intricately linked to emotional issues that are not at first glance terribly obvious. We knew that if we could get behind the words dependency, love, nurturance, wanting and insecurity, we might be able to understand something central about women's (and men's) experience. In our practice we continually heard of our clients' insecurities, whether that was expressed through jealousy, competition, envy or mistrust of others. Inside each woman was a part of herself that was isolated, hidden, felt abandoned, rejected and infantile. We had to ask ourselves, if society directs women to be dependent why do they feel so insecure about others being there for them; if it's all right for women to be dependent why does it take months in the therapy for a woman client to begin to let us see the dependent part of herself? Over the past decade on both sides of the Atlantic this theme of dependency seemed to be at the very core of women's psychology.

The embryo of the theme of dependency began to emerge early on in our clinical work. In those years we

discussed our findings that women had a great deal of
difficulty in receiving attention in the therapy relationship.
Being listened to, taken seriously and related to with
empathy and care was obviously an unfamiliar position for a
woman to be in. We noticed that a client would make
attempts to reciprocate the care and attention of the
therapist, that after three or four sessions she would feel that
perhaps she had had enough of what she was needing. We
began to see that client after client experienced discomfort
in digesting the possibility that we genuinely were interested
in what she had to say and who she was. She found it equally
difficult to believe that care and concern was authentic. It
became clear that a woman could listen to others, give
attention to others, be on the giving side of a relationship
with an ease that she could not come near when on the
receiving end. In short, we began to notice that, far from
the popular belief that women were dependent on others,
in fact women strongly protected themselves against showing their dependency needs. Women expressed feelings of
shame and self-dislike for having these needs in the first
place. Time and again we heard our clients assuming that
they should not and could not expect care and attention
from anyone else; that they should be able to take care of
themselves; that needing equalled weakness and childish-
ness. At the same time they spoke of their assumptions that
they had to be available to respond to the needs of others.
The imbalance glared out at us. This need to give and the
difficulty with receiving was such a feature of each woman
we encountered that we began to see it as central to the
development of women's psychology. When we shared our
observations of this phenomenon with women in groups
they sighed with recognition and the realization of this as
not just a personal issue but one which touched us all. As
theme after theme began to be unravelled in discussion,
women saw themselves in each other and felt both relief and
closeness with each other. The various barriers that had
divided women's experiences seemed to disappear as
mothers, daughters, grandmothers, teenagers, middle-class

women, working-class women, lesbians and heterosexual women felt each other's pain so identified with their own. We were continually struck at how emotionally similar women's lives were, regardless of individual life situations, Our views on the theme of dependency are continually confirmed by the many women we talk to and see clinically.

In this book we have tried to include the experiences of all the women we have worked with. This means that you will meet women of different ages — some of them married, some single, some living with other women. Their openness enabled us to assemble the kaleidoscope of experience that makes up the many different facets of dependency we present here. We gratefully appreciate what we have learnt from our clients and hope that our current understanding of women's and men's psychology, its interplay and consequences for couple relationships and women's friendships will resonate for you.

We would like to thank Henrietta Heald for thoughtful editing.

LUISE EICHENBAUM
SUSIE ORBACH
London and New York

1

Exploding the Myth of Dependency

It is now over fifty years since Freud threw up his hands in exasperation over the question of what women want. Since then, psychoanalysts, humanists, researchers of human relationships and, of course, women and men have also pondered this question. Defined by others, and for so long living in the shadow of men, women themselves have only recently articulated their desires, their wants and their most intimate thoughts. Men, meanwhile, have been perplexed by women's demands. Because men's and women's socialization and daily life experience are very different, it often feels as if women live in one emotional world and men in another. The separateness of these worlds can cause terrible consequences when a man and a woman become intimately involved with one another: at present we are witnessing a new crisis in male-female relationships. But what makes women and men tick is not really so different. We will show that what makes it so hard for them to relate satisfactorily is a deep confusion and misunderstanding over the dependency needs of themselves and each other.

The thread of dependency runs through all human relationships — modern marriage is itself a complex mix of dependency, sexuality and autonomy. While popular myth tells us that women are dependent and men independent, a turn of the axis puts a radically different light on women's and men's dependency needs and gratifications. For too long we have laboured under the myth that men are big and strong and independent; that women are passive, helpless and dependent. Yet the attempts of the women's liberation movement to break these stereotypes have all too often

floundered on the limitations that women themselves feel to
be a part of their emotional make-up. Why?

In this book, we begin to answer this question by
proposing a radically new way to view women's and men's
emotional dependency. It emerges from our clinical practice as psychotherapists, where we investigated the intimate
thoughts and feelings of hundreds of women clients and of
couples, and discovered time and again emotional similar-
ities. In love affairs, marriages and close relationships with
men, women discussed how they could rarely sustain the
deep emotional connection they longed for. Moreover, in
their disappointments in love, they were forced to confront
another, and often previously obscured, aspect of their
personalities. They found that their emotional lives had
become overwhelmingly wrapped up in a search for contact
and understanding from their mates. They had become
'clingy'. Men, meanwhile, felt frustrated, bewildered and
confused about what their partners wanted. What *do*
women want?

Colette Dowling's *Cinderella Complex*, published in
Britain in 1982, struck a resounding chord in today's women
because, for perhaps the first time, it brought this crucial
issue of dependency into the open. However, while her case
studies are accurate, Dowling lacks the psychoanalytic or
clinical understanding to draw the correct conclusions. Her
thesis — that progress towards equality of the sexes is
hampered by the learned dependency that goes with
growing up female — misses, from our perspective, the
central point at issue.

Dependency is not, as Colette Dowling suggests, 'the
refusal to accept responsibility'. It is a basic human need.
Psychological development theorists and psychotherapeutic
practitioners know that achieving autonomy and independence rests on the *gratification* of dependency needs. It is
only when a child feels confident that she or he *can* depend
on others that the child grows up feeling confident enough to
be independent. Women are indeed fearful of independence
and success, but this is not because they have been raised to

depend on others. On the contrary, women are raised to be depended *upon*; to place their emotional needs second to those of others. While women have traditionally been dependent economically, they have always been the emotional caretakers of the family. At the same time as women are depended upon for emotional support and nurturance, they learn to *behave* dependently. Girls learn from very early on that it is dependent behaviour (passivity, helplessness, submissiveness) which will get them what they are searching for — i.e. someone to care for them consistently. However, it is important to distinguish between the ways in which women *behave* dependently ('I can't screw this screw into the wall') and women's true emotional dependency *needs* ('I need someone who will understand me and love me').

In confusing economic and emotional dependency, Colette Dowling assumes, first, that women's emotional dependency needs are satisfactorily met. This does not match with our own clinical findings, for if these needs are met why do women continue to have complicated feelings about them? Second, she suggests that women should be more like men, without taking into account the ways in which, in an unacknowledged way, men rely on women. She does not address the fact that men's emotional dependency needs are, in fact, more consistently catered to than women's and that this fact has a direct correlation to men's ability to be more 'independent'. Dowling tends to confirm what most women feel and fear: that is, their dependency needs signify weakness. Our account offers a deeper analysis of this phenomenon.

Over the past thirteen years, since the second wave of twentieth-century feminism got into its stride, thousands and thousands of women have attempted to tackle the problem of dependency. They know that it is a critical theme in their day-to-day lives — it is woven into the very fabric of their experience of what it means to be a woman. It is only recently that we are coming to understand that liberation does not mean an 'independence' achieved through emotional isolation, of not needing from others. Women must throw off the dependent behaviour traits and stereotypes that cripple them, but ultimately this will only be possible when they receive gratification of their own needs. This means that men as well as women have an enormous task in front of them.

In our culture, both men and women come to feel ashamed of feeling dependent. It seems to signify weakness in both sexes but in different ways. Boys grow up on the other side of an unbalanced coin. Their dependency needs are hidden from view, but more successfully answered. A boy grows up learning to depend on women, first his mother and then his wife. A girl grows up learning she will have to give up her mother without getting wifely love in its place. Paradoxically, precisely because men have the continuity that women are denied, male needs are less exposed. Women and men collude in this process of keeping from view men's dependency needs. The true picture of women's and men's dependency on each other is not acknowledged.

Throughout our lives, we depend on other people for our emotional growth and well-being. Society is an intricate network of economic and emotional relationships. Within this network, the roles that women and men take up are very different, and the psychological roads we must travel in growing up reflect this. As psychotherapists, we are concerned with the cultural experiences that shape our sense of ourselves as feminine or masculine. Brothers and sisters raised in the same family are subject to radically different socialization. They are the recipients of different kinds of attention, different kinds of touching and holding, different instructions, different language, different attitudes and different expectations. We are all aware of how, in obvious ways, sex-role stereotyping has affected us, and that it influences how we rear our children. Generally speaking, girls are supposed to be sweet and demure, boys are supposed to be active and brave. What we might be less clear about is how our deeply personal concerns, anxieties and insecurities are also a reflection of this same phenomenon.

How we relate to the great themes of love, hate, desire, self-expression, closeness and separateness, and how we experience our disappointments, our pleasures, our needs and hopes being met or not met, or our entitlement to our desires, mirror in complex ways what we have experienced in our early development. In other words, boys and girls are, if you like, motivated in subtly different ways emotionally.

Our relationships are guided from the first day of our lives by the conscious and unconscious sense that our parents, grandparents, aunts, uncles, sisters, brothers, nursery school teachers, have of their own and our gender.[1] Gender permeates to the deepest reaches of ourselves. Many of the central aspects of our personality development are shaped by whether we are girls or boys. Girls and boys do not have radically different emotional lives from the start; rather, our inner experiences are honed in ways that are related to our gender. We grow up with the idea that men must be and are independent, strong, able and competent. A man who feels himself to be lacking essential 'masculine' attributes can come to feel inadequate and uncomfortable. A woman, we learn, must be nurturing, involved in a relationship and attractive. A woman who doesn't see herself this way can feel like a freak.

When we look deep into women's and men's psyches to

1. The construction of gender identity starts at birth. All those who interact with the infant are aware of its biological sex and this is manifest in subtle and obvious ways as it grows. One of the most profound ways we come to know ourselves is as either a girl or a boy — i.e. as feminine or masculine — and the work of psychologists John Money and Anke Erhardt shows that the attributes we associate with femininity or masculinity are cultural constructions. See J. Money and A. Erhardt, *Man and Woman, Boy and Girl: the differentiation and dimorphism of gender identity from conception to maturity*, Baltimore 1972, London 1973. For a discussion of the importance of gender identity in psychological development see L. Eichenbaum and S. Orbach, *Outside In, Inside Out: Women's Psychology, a feminist psychoanalytic approach*, London 1982.

see what really makes up a woman and what makes up a man, we find emotional states that are dramatically different from the patterns that appear on the surface. Men are brought up to display their independence and separateness. But we discover, in fact, that men are quite hesitant, even afraid, to disclose that they feel emotionally dependent. They will often resist such an idea or retreat from an examination of their inner needs with vehemence. A basic protective mechanism is at work here. People develop a defensive stance when they fear (unconsciously) a threat to their conception of self, the loss of something felt as important, or as a protection against a painful or unpleasant idea. When men shy away from exploring this issue, they may well be trying not to disturb the rather precarious view of dependency that has been instilled in them. But behind the display lives another self. A self who is vulnerable, dependent and capable of being tremendously hurt. A person who counts on a woman — be it mother, a lover, a wife or a girlfriend — to be there for them, to be concerned about their emotional well-being; a woman whom the man leans on and relies on for a certain kind of emotional caretaking and nurturance.

All of us are utterly dependent in infancy. In the course of our development we become more and more physically adept, while our personalities form and take shape in the context of family relationships. More than likely, the little boy starts off life dependent on his mother, who will often be his sole caretaker. If he goes to a crèche or is looked after by other family members, they will usually be female. A boy comes to know dependency in relation to women. It is women who have the power to comfort him or, as he may perceive it at times, withhold it from him. From the arms of mother, sister, aunt or grandmother, the boy leaves home to another environment shaped by a woman, the kindergarten or nursery school, and to another woman, the female teacher. The authority figure, the nurturing person, the central persons in his world, are female. As the boy grows up, he and those around him anticipate a future which means that he will always have a close relationship with a woman. Eventually he will be able to bring his emotional life and his dependency needs into a marriage. *His needs for emotional nurturance are addressed without him having actively to confront them or spell them out.* This is the background against which he hears the various injunctions and rules about masculinity. His father, peers, teachers and the women around him introduce him to the elements of sex-role stereotyping, of learning how to be a man, hide his emotions, keep up a good front, develop confidence, project independent and courageous attributes. Hidden from view then, and presented even in their opposite form, as we shall see, are men's dependency needs. Every woman knows that men rely on them and that the idea that men are independent and women dependent is essentially a false one.

A girl grows up knowing that she is expected to marry a man for whom she will provide nurturance, care and emotional support, and bring into the world children who will depend on her. Just like the little boy, the little girl's personality develops in a predominantly female ambiance. She, like her brother, depends first on her mother and then on other women for her emotional and physical growth. But as she becomes an adult the female's life will take a dramatic shift: she must prepare herself for the demands of marriage. The sex-role stereotyping imposed on females means that girls are encouraged to grow up learning to modify or squash their impulses towards independence and self-expression.

A girl may develop tentative and clingy behaviour. She *appears* dependent, incompetent and somewhat fragile. She learns to look outside herself for guidance and leadership. But behind this outward façade is someone who, whatever her inner state, will have to deal with the emotional problems met in family relationships, a person who knows that others will expect to rely and lean on her, a person who fears that she will never really be able to depend on others or never feels content about her dependency.

These roles that women and men develop can exact a tremendous emotional cost. They may deprive us of feeling good, safe and expansive. The patriarchal system shapes our sense of gender, and consequently who we feel we are, in damaging ways. How women relate to men, how men relate to women and how women relate to each other reveal extra-ordinarily complicated patterns of dependency needs which are hidden, distorted and rarely talked about or met straight-forwardly. In our work as psychotherapists, seeing women on their own and heterosexual couples, we have come to the startling conclusion that while girls and women are raised to display dependent behaviour — or perhaps it would be more correctly labelled 'deference behaviour', a looking up to the man — they are cautioned against showing their real emotional needs. *Girls absorb early on that in the most profound sense they must rely on themselves, there is no one to take care of them emotionally.* They *cannot* assume — as does the man — that there will be someone for them to bring their emotional lives to.

The ability to depend on others is crucial to growth and development. A child needs to feel that it can depend on the adults it is close to. For it is only when a child feels confident that she or he *can* depend on others that the child can develop with the security and confidence that allows one to become independent. A child, male or female, who grows up with this kind of experience can more easily look forward to life outside the family with excitement, with the ex-pectation of fitting in, with confidence that new experiences will be enriching. A child who has been sufficiently nur-tured, who knows that it is loved for itself, who can depend on its parents for genuine support, approaches life in a spirit of assurance. It will find the world full of inviting and satisfying relationships and projects. A child who has not had this kind of introduction to life will feel more insecure and on some level will always be searching for the contact it missed and now craves. The world will seem more complex, and fearful.

In our society, too few people receive the kind of

nurturance that allows them to get the best out of new relationships. Our early relationships can be fraught with disappointment and misunderstanding. So many of us live with a missing piece inside, a confusion and worry; we yearn for a soulmate who will love us, understand us and help us face ourselves.

But, as we shall see, what men and women need, the sort of emotional involvement they seek, reflect the differences in their upbringing.

The need for nurturance and emotional fulfilment stays with us throughout life. When we are understood and responded to, we feel more whole within ourselves and the world. Emotional involvement sustains us mentally just as the meals we eat and the air we breathe sustain us physically. Without it we suffer privation.

The difference between women's and men's dependency needs is something that we are just beginning to see and understand more clearly because the patterns we all grew up with are changing. Our society is engaged in a huge transformation in sexual relationships. Only ten years ago most women had their babies early in their twenties. Many women worked outside the home, but still saw their central identity as linked to their family. Today many more women work outside the home, many heads of households are female, and women are marrying later, and postponing having children.

These are dramatic changes to have occurred in such a short space of time. They have touched all our lives, directly or indirectly. We all know women and men who are choosing to live on their own; many of us know homosexual couples; many of us know women who have chosen not to have children; and we all know women who are now able to support themselves economically. At the same time that options for women have been expanding, men's traditional role in the family has been threatened. Men are being dislodged from their position as the primary breadwinners[2]

2. This has been an economic fiction for a long time, although still
    widely believed.

both by the worsening economic situation and by women's changing role. Consequently what women and men bring to marriage and intimate relationships, and what they look for in them, could be expected to have changed equally dramatically. In fact, while women may not look to men to support them economically or to provide them with legitimacy for being sexual, and while men may not automatically assume the role of breadwinner, many aspects of what we seek in a love partner are only changing very very slowly. The changes in all of us at a private and emotional level have not kept pace with the broad changes in family arrangements. These societal changes are allowing us to peek behind the veil of marriage to the political nature of the transactions in our intimate relationships. Now that so many more women are sharing the economic costs of raising a family, certain emotional transactions that were not obvious before become dramatically apparent. It is as though the overwhelming need for a husband to provide economic support and sexual legitimacy screened out the flaws and discrepancies in the emotional exchanges between a husband and wife. With the disintegration of this veil the dissatisfactions in intimate relationships are emerging. Ruth no longer stays with Harry because, despite the lack of intimacy, closeness and feelings of friendship, 'he's a good man, I never had to ask for anything materially'. Ruth feels frustrated, cheated and aggrieved. Harry, who has given what he knows how to give — a nice house, steady participation in the community, and worked hard to provide a good standard of living — is perplexed. 'What *does* she want?'

This book was written to address that question and to enable us to understand how intimate relationships work today so that we can transform our relationships the better to meet our needs. We are at once writing about what is and arguing for what could be. We interweave theory with the stories of women and men we have met in the course of our work as psychotherapists. We are describing the lives of individual women and men but the issues that affect them apply to women and men across class and ethnic backgrounds. We are examining the impact of child-rearing arrangements where by and large mothers raise children; at the same time, we plead for an urgent restructuring of domestic arrangements. We concentrate on the mother-daughter and mother-son relationship, for it is primarily women who raise children, but we argue for the involvement of men in the care of children from infancy on. We are describing the structure of relating in most heterosexual relationships, because we have all experienced the pressure to have our sexuality conform to our societal arrangements, but we passionately believe in a freer sexuality that allows for love between women and women, men and men, and men and women. What we describe in these pages are painful themes that arise, we believe, as a result of our gendered arrangements. We hope that the reader, in seeing herself or himself on the page, will recognize how deeply gender shapes her or his emotional life and the ways in which we relate. We hope that the struggles of the women and men we describe provide both a sense of optimism and one of urgency about the needs to address these issues in order for us to relate more fully.

2

Forbidden Feelings: Women and Dependency

> 'All I want is to know that someone is
> *really* there for me; then I know I could
> relax and go off and do my own thing.'

Helen is twenty-seven, a bookkeeper and unmarried. She used to live with Bob but they broke up two years ago. Since then she has gone out with a lot of men. We see her now getting ready to go out for the first time properly with Paul, a thirty-five year old divorced social worker whom she met a week before on a blind date. It is Saturday evening and Helen is lounging in her bath, steaming her face before the big event. The afternoon was spent buying new shoes, belt and a scarf to complete tonight's outfit. She's been so excited by the date, she's hardly eaten all day. She is savouring the possibility that they will 'fall in love' and have a wonderful time together. Already she has fantasies of meeting his parents, of introducing him to hers, of the summer vacation filled with gins and tonics and him on a Greek island....

Six months later Paul and Helen were seeing each other regularly. Their relationship had already lost its glitter. Helen was frustrated and disappointed and she was worried about how Paul spent the evenings that they were apart. She got very clingy and felt things would be much better if they lived together. She had become particularly jealous of Renata, a workmate of Paul's, and imagined that Paul and Renata enjoyed each other's company more than she and Paul did. Secretly she feared that Paul would leave her for Renata, who was more interesting, more attractive, more everything Paul could possibly want, as Helen saw it.

Helen was desperate for attachment but unaware of how

difficult it was for her and how afraid of it she was. The emptiness she felt drove her to dream up an elaborate fantasy life. Before their first date, Paul had already been the knight on the white charger who would arrive and make sense of her life. Helen had no inner conception of her substance and strength. She had been brought up to live a life that could be jettisoned or suspended when the right man came along. She had been discouraged from carving out the shape of a life that would suit or reflect who *she* was. This became evident to her through quite minor issues, which struck her as curious. When she had broken up with Bob she had become obsessed, for example, about the kind of cutlery she should buy, unsure of what she really liked, and yet she pondered on how opinionated and sure of her design ideas she had been when she lived with Bob. Then, she had known just what she had wanted and hadn't been afraid to act on her ideas. Because she felt unable to construct a real life for herself when she was on her own, Helen came to live increasingly in a fantasy world, one over which she could have some control. She daydreamed about a world that no one else could touch, where relationships worked out as planned, as in films, a world in which she felt safer and more secure. This retreat into her inner world made her look at what was actually going on in her life with a rather skewed vision. She attributed the distance between herself and Paul to another woman, Renata. But Paul had never been interested in a sexual relationship with Renata and was confused by Helen's jealousy. Helen had conjured up Renata as a threat to explain to herself the difficulties between herself and Paul. Much as she longed for closeness and intimacy, she did not believe that she could trust Paul. Her desperate need for security and connection, coupled with the fantasy world she was living in, meant that when she was faced with a real relationship which *did* offer security, *she did not know how to cope with it.* She was unable to trust Paul and saw (false) evidence of his desertion and his desire to get away from her at any point. She lived on tenterhooks, convinced that the emotional axe would fall and that she would be in the cold again.

*   *   *

Katie did not marry until she was thirty-seven, a year after meeting Pete on a trip to Europe. She had a very independent existence up to that time, working for the B.B.C. She had resisted lots of subtle and not so subtle pressures to marry sooner. She was determined not to settle, but to wait until she met a man who would stir up strong, passionate and loving feelings in her. For the first two years of their relationship Pete and she lived in a kind of honeymoon bliss. They returned from their jobs eager to see each other and with lots of energy left over to talk, walk, make love, visit friends. In the third year of being together Katie, after long talks and planning with Pete, gave up her job and decided to risk going freelance. She was very nervous about making the break from a safe and tenured job at a time of economic insecurity, especially as Pete earned quite a bit less than she (they did not share money but they split the common expenses down the middle). But she was really fed up at work and wanted the challenge of starting up on her own. At the same time as she decided to make the break, Pete, a union shop steward, was coincidentally sent away on a week's course at short notice. Katie felt totally abandoned and wondered how she was going to make it through an entire week without him. She was frantically busy tidying up the loose ends at work. In fact, she only had one free night in the whole week. And yet she felt dejected, rejected, vulnerable and scared at the thought of being on her own. Pete returned from the week wrung out and tired. He behaved in a withdrawn and distant way and it emerged later that he was actually feeling lousy about having left Katie for the week. Shortly after his return he got a cold, then he had an accident playing football. He was laid up at home for several weeks. Katie looked after him and was a tower of strength. He gradually got better but something significant in their relationship changed from that point on. For the next few years, Katie felt suspicious towards Pete and somewhat disdainful. She felt he couldn't really give to her in the way he had in the past and she wondered whether she was right about what had originally flowed between them. But at the same time as she became somewhat contemptuous of him and even undermined his attempts to reach out to her, she became increasingly dependent on the relationship and felt more insecure than she had for ages. She kept looking to Pete for some sign that he still loved her and wanted her.

Katie discovered with an unpleasant jolt that she could not rely on maintaining an independent stance while she was in a close relationship. As soon as she had opened herself up in this relationship all her hidden and forbidden dependency desires came up and overwhelmed her. She was caught out by the intensity of her feelings of abandonment and rage at Pete. And she resented being so affected by these emotions. She'd been in women's groups and thought she had got over such disabling feelings. Her leaving work, combined with the untimely separation, meant that she was out on her own without Pete's support. She had experienced enormous conflict about her decision to go freelance and felt awful when the volume of incoming work was lower than her target. She became very sensitive to feelings of rejection.

The unfortunate sequence of events had destabilized Katie. Nerves had been touched and her self-confidence shattered. The explanation for this went back years before Katie was involved with Pete. From beneath the layers of rationality and life experience, Katie's unconscious asserted itself. With different players and different goals, Katie was reliving with Pete her very earliest childhood steps towards independence.

When we first come into the world we are utterly dependent. Without food, physical care or emotional sustenance we cannot grow. Emotional connection is such an important feature of our survival that babies taken into care but given no love and personal attention cannot sustain life — they give up and die.[1] Whoever cares for us first and most consistently — usually our mother — becomes our

1. Rene A. Spitz, *The First Year of Life: A Psychoanalytic Study of Normal and Deviant Development of Object Relations*, New York 1965.

psychological umbilical cord. We depend on her for our very existence. We are merged with her and have no sense of where we begin or where she ends. What she gives us emotionally forms the very essence of our personality. Her love and attention is an essential food that builds our personality. It is as important as the physical nurture we receive to develop our bodies. She fills up our world, and our first experiences, pleasurable and painful, take place in an emotional context which she has created. We are enraptured by her, fascinated by and very much in need of her.

If she is enthusiastic about other people, this enthusiasm will be communicated to us and we will be eager to make other relationships. A mother who is anxious will communicate that anxiety and her children will face new relationships with unease and uncertainty.

Every mother has the almost impossible task of juggling her needs and the needs of her child. Every mother feels conflict about her child's dependency on her, both enjoying and resenting it. Every mother worries about whether she is giving too much or too little. Every mother knows there are times when her child needs her desperately and times when she must let go. Every western twentieth-century mother has absorbed enough popular psychology to feel responsible for the mental health of her child. A mother's care and attention builds the foundation from which her child moves into the larger world. As the child is able to move around physically it explores the world around itself, it lets its mother know that it needs her in different ways. The physical growth goes hand in hand with changes in emotional development. The child gravitates towards other people, it begins to look to them to fulfil some of the needs that its mother provided before. The toddler is taking its first steps in the process of separating and becoming its own person. This is a process that occurs all through life but developmental psychologists have observed three or four distinct periods, such as adolescence, leaving home and starting a family, in which as children and adults we take a sort of emotional stock and try and move forward into some different emotional alignment. The first of these periods occurs between eighteen and thirty months. Psychologists refer to it as 'separation-individuation'.[2] The child, who has embodied a reasonable degree of caring from its mother or mother substitute, begins to feel its own boundaries, its own sense of self, its own differences from this big person who is always present. It begins to experiment with feeling this new sense of 'me', of checking out its impact on the environment, of feeling its separateness from its mother. The way it approaches the larger world will depend enormously on what it has absorbed up until this time. Some children are very enthusiastic, others tentative or fearful, and others pursue new experiences with almost wild abandon. What happens when the child is establishing its separateness affects how the next new encounter will be approached. With every attempt to explore, the emotional image of mother is present... it is she that the child is distinguishing itself from, and it is she to whom the child returns to reassure itself, to refuel, to touch home base.

When children make precocious attempts to separate from their mother or, later on in the adolescent phase of separation, from their family, we have to ask what is going on, what is propelling them out of the nest ... is it enough nurturance, plenty to feed on so that they are satisfied early; or is it that there is not enough of the right kind of nurturance and they need to seek it elsewhere; or is it perhaps that being merged itself was too sticky and cloying, not really satisfying?

In Katie's case, as we shall see with so many women, her apparent adult independence was a version of a survival tool she had developed when she was very little, while she was going through the stage of separation-individuation. Katie's mother was herself rather insecure and after Katie's birth found it tremendously difficult to be responsive to her

2. Margaret S. Mahler, Fred Pure, and Anni Bergman, *The Psychological Birth of the Human Infant: Symbiosis and Individuation*, New York and London 1975.

daughter. It was almost as though she felt jealous of the very attention her daughter demanded. She wanted someone to be giving to her, in an adult version, what she was giving to Katie. Katie's father, a busy doctor, seemed to have more time for his patients than for his wife or daughter. Katie's mother had become rather self-absorbed in her pregnancy, and her husband, feeling somewhat shut out, had retreated into building his practice and his reputation. Katie's mother felt exhausted. She longed to weep although she couldn't really say why. She felt tremendous urges to collapse but knew that her responsibilities towards her husband and Katie meant that she couldn't and she shouldn't. She tried to take herself in hand and suppress all her feelings of weakness and upset. She tried to be a good mother and attend to Katie's needs. But Katie's needs frightened her, *for they reminded her of her own forbidden feelings*. Sometimes she was unable to be responsive to Katie, to tune in absolutely to what she wanted and, in giving to her, provide a reassurance that all was well. At other times, Katie's mother ignored her needs, just as she was forced to ignore her own. The situation would then escalate, with the mother feeling less and less patient, less and less able to give Katie what she needed. Katie might get distraught, her mother would not know what to do.

It was from this kind of insecure atmosphere that Katie made her first attempts at separation at age two. She showed her 'independence' in many ways. She tied her own shoe laces, she fed herself, and as she got older she insisted that she walk to school on her own, that she prepare her own lunches and so on. These displays of 'independence' in fact hid her real needs. At the same time she (unconsciously) discovered another way of hiding her own needs. She began to look after the needs of others, particularly those of her father. Attending to others and denying her own needs was encouraged by everyone around her. One day when she was feeling miserable and let her mother see her unhappiness, her mother responded by suggesting Katie bake a cake for her dad. 'Daddy will be so pleased.' Katie was a good girl.

She was never *selfish*. She was so giving and thoughtful of others. Katie by this time had absorbed both the loving aspects of her mother's care and the confusing ones. She was a little girl who had inadmissible needs now hidden inside her. She made an unconscious resolution to approach the bigger world without the cumbersome neediness of her first years. She couldn't bear to feel the rejection again. For, when her mother had ignored her or become frustrated with her, Katie had not understood what was going on, had only felt its impact and she had had to make sense of her mother's actions. Katie came to understand that she shouldn't rely on her mother too much, that she should 'grow up' as fast as she could, or at least hide away her little-girl part. In quashing this part of herself, Katie grew up making the equation that there was something vaguely wrong with what she wanted and with her needs.

When she began to look outside the mother-daughter orbit during the period of separation-individuation, she was hoping either to have her needs met elsewhere or escape them altogether. Of course none of this was conscious, either on her mother's part or on Katie's. In Katie's inner world she resolved to bury the dependent, wanting part of her forever. She thrust forward, taking up challenges with gusto, proving to herself that she could handle different situations. Every new situation built her confidence that she could cope, that she could take care of herself, that she didn't really need anyone. But every victory had its reverse psychic effect, for Katie became more and more distant from the little-girl part of her inside who had stopped growing, whose needs had been prematurely nipped in the bud, who still hungered for consistent attention. The little-girl part did not present itself directly, indeed she might never have become reacquainted with her if she had found enough challenges to negate her existence. But when Katie fell in love with Pete, a part of her psyche unfroze. The woman with tight and rigid boundaries melted a bit and she let another person have a fundamental impact on her. In her closeness with Pete, her earlier feelings of closeness with her mother were re-evoked — both the positive and the difficult experiences. When Pete 'left her' for the week at a point when she was moving out of her secure job at the B.B.C., she felt as though she was being abandoned to face the world once again on her own. More than that even, she unconsciously felt as though his departure was some kind of punishment for her new work decision. Inside Katie, his trip took on a different meaning. Katie felt that she was utterly unsupported, could not rely on Pete any more, and that in some profound way, by his leaving at this point, the emotional cradle they had created was irrevocably ripped. When he returned and seemed distant, and then fell ill, Katie 'knew' for sure she had been right. She was resentful that Pete was so wrapped up in himself that he was unaware that she was going through a difficult time. She felt she couldn't express her anxieties and fears about changing her job because his needs were so present. Katie felt she should never have let herself get that close to a man: they only disappoint you just when you need them. She found herself having to look after him at a time when she was feeling she would like that bit of reassurance herself. She felt he became terribly dependent in a rather indirect way, just at the point when she was needing his support to take on a new challenge in a different way. His illness put her into an old role of competently caring for another while having to suppress her own needs.

When she came to one of our workshops on dependency to discuss the whole situation, she became aware of how disappointed and upset she was about the course of events. She realized that she didn't want Pete to do very much at all; she didn't really want to collapse, and felt she could conquer any challenge if she only knew that he was really behind her. Until that fateful week and the ensuing illness she had felt Pete was really there for her, concerned about her. She experienced his week's absence as a withdrawal and a rejection. It flung her back almost thirty-five years to feelings of utter loneliness and anxiety that she had suppressed. She felt that she had been dropped, she had been pushed out rather than gone forward from choice and with loving support. She was forced to deny her dependency needs once again. These needs were so forbidden.

Margaret was widowed at sixty-eight. For forty years she had described her marriage as miserable, her husband as ungiving and her life as one experience after another of not getting what she wanted. For forty years she had led a fairly 'independent' life, going out to work, attending meetings, travelling to see friends. She had long given up entertaining at home. She wasn't much of a grandmother to her only granddaughter. For forty years she shared a bedroom with a man who 'grunted at her', showed little affection and even less interest in her life. For forty years she dreaded the almost daily skirmishes, the anguish, and the lack of joy in her marital life.

When Robert died, her world collapsed. She stopped eating, cooking or shopping and spent her days gazing at the TV set. He left her comfortably off but she couldn't feel secure. Each day she clenched her bank book, called her accountant and counted her pennies. Her children, alarmed at the change in her, asked what was wrong. 'Now that your father has gone, there is no point,' she said with bitterness.

At twenty-four, after graduating from college and teaching for two years, Margaret had left her parents' home in New York to marry a talented Englishman, Robert, a professor of linguistics at London University. The idea of marriage to a foreigner had heightened the romantic flavour of the courtship for each of them. To a New York middle-class young woman, London and an Englishman spelled culture, excitement, history and grace. Margaret saw her life unfolding with bigger horizons. Like many women of her background, Margaret had grown up at a time and in an atmosphere which directed young women to seek to satisfy their ambitions by marrying interesting men. An exciting life meant marrying a man who had himself an exciting life. Her pleasure was to come through sharing his joys and ambitions and by together overcoming his problems.

Margaret approached her wedding with tremendous eagerness and joy.

If we look at Margaret's story with fresh eyes, new insights
challenge the basis of this old perspective, allowing us to see
how the complex theme of dependency plays out in this
relationship.

We discover a familiar story. Robert was the recipient, at
least early on in the marriage, of Margaret's care and
attentiveness towards his career and general concerns. In
fact there were two people 'working on' and committed to
his having the fullest life possible. Margaret was not in a
parallel position. Her own career ambitions were slowly
dropped. Margaret wanted to be a lawyer but such a
training in England in the 1930s was closed to those who did
not have the social connections made at English private
schools and the money to support a long apprenticeship. She
received no support from Robert's family for her attempt at
a career as they were not much taken with the idea of a
woman seeking a profession. Their opinion echoed that of
many of her contemporaries and Margaret found that she
was somewhat at odds with Robert's friends, who felt a
woman should regard her family as her central activity.
Robert himself was concerned that Margaret find something
interesting to do until they started a family. Margaret's
teaching qualifications were not accepted in England and
for the next several years she drifted into and out of fairly
boring work in interesting fields. She was a secretary to an
anti-fascist organization, then to a cultural group who were
putting on avant-garde musicals. She was frustrated, felt
somewhat cheated, missed her friends terribly and saw
England turn grey before her eyes. Meanwhile, her relationship with Robert seemed to be deteriorating. They were
squabbling quite a bit and she felt continually pushed aside.
She longed to go back to America, to her family and friends
and to law school, but Robert was reluctant to leave
England. He felt a bit guilty about her situation and didn't
exactly know how to help her. But sadly he was unable to
reveal how he felt to her, and instead he retreated away from

her pain and upset. Margaret, for her part, felt hurt, rejected and abandoned. A part of her tried to accept the situation, a part of her made calculations — 'I gave up so much to be here with him, and now he has the nerve to withdraw from me.' A part of her turned bitter and resentful. She felt her life to be a bit of a disappointment, she loved Robert just as much but she didn't feel he really understood her that well. She herself was worried that she was becoming a nag, someone who couldn't be satisfied.

Eventually Margaret had two children, a son and a daughter, born during the war. Robert was in the air force and for safety she took the children to the United States, to her mother's home. She was very happy to be back in New York with family and friends. She felt they understood what she'd been going through in England, and they encouraged her to stay in New York.

But Margaret felt deeply tied to Robert. The physical distance between them brought out their love and concern for each other strongly. They wrote to each other frequently and both looked forward to the end of the war and their reunion. As the time for Robert's release grew closer, Margaret fantasized about the happy family they would create and share. Her expectation of being together again, with the bumps behind them, excited her. She found herself longing to be with Robert and she got on the first passenger boat that would take her.

Within six months it was clear that the marriage was in trouble. Robert was an attentive father but not such an attentive husband. He devoted more and more of his spare time to causes and to his work. She wondered what she was doing wrong. Margaret craved more togetherness but was inevitably disappointed. Their sex life deteriorated and they fought regularly and with increasing bitterness. Every day Margaret resolved not to want so much from him. Every day she talked to herself about not being so dissatisfied, but every day she found herself hatching plans to go back home, seeing if she could muster the strength inside her to leave him. Every day she felt like a failure — she couldn't whole-

heartedly stay and she couldn't leave. Her visiting girl
friends urged her to get a divorce but all she could say was,
'What will become of me, I need him so!'

So why did Margaret stay in this disappointing marriage?
She was lonely, cut off from her roots and her support
systems, and increasingly miserable. We can begin to
answer this dilemma by asking what really made her leave
America in the first place. How was it that she came to be so
attracted to a man who lived 3000 miles away that she would
jettison contact with her friends, her family, and give up
having a career?

Margaret idealized her mother. To her, Shirley was
wonderful and uncriticizable. But to Robert and other
observers, Shirley was in reality a self-involved and selfish
woman. While she led a very active social life and was much
loved by her friends, she had a rather distant relationship
with her husband and children. She rarely let their needs
stand in her way. She expected the three children to look
after each other and she played with them only occasionally,
on a whim. Margaret learned an awful lot about coping
with her own problems early on. Occasionally she would
turn to her older sister for advice and comfort but essentially the two girls became women long before their time.
The sisters were much admired for their independence and
felt very proud that so much of the care of their little
brother was entrusted to them. They were praised for being
ever such good mummies. But why did Margaret carry
around this strong image that her mother was so wonderful?
Why did she call out for her in her sleep for years after her
death?

The strong positive image that Margaret carried of her
mother covered up a complex of painful, contradictory
feelings that Margaret had towards Shirley deep inside. In
fact Margaret's childhood experiences were punctuated by
hurt, disappointment, anger and a sense of abandonment.
Shirley was not that attentive, available or nurturing. She
was very involved with her work and committees, and was
not very comfortable with her children and related to them

rather inconsistently. They were very much her achievements, and were required to be attractive, polite, and
responsive children. Behind this description of them was the
psychological cost of their achieving this perfection.
Margaret was a child who was discouraged from showing
her needs. When she cried, her mother would say, 'That's
enough now.' When she complained about being unhappy,
her mother implied that things couldn't be *that* bad.
Margaret grew up hiding the part of her that was miserable,
confused, tearful and needy and developed a pleasing
outside personality that mother was more prepared to relate
to. Margaret's 'outer personality' was capable and charming
and other people responded warmly to her. The little-girl
part was now quite at odds with Margaret's self-image and
Margaret herself was unaware of how her early experiences
shaped what she was hoping for and expecting in her adult
relationships.

Margaret's brother Eddie had a rather different experience in adult life. Being the recipient of his two sisters' caring
and of much more attention from his mother than either of
them had received, he was a boy who grew up feeling loved,
entitled to love and with a fairly strong expectation that he
would have love in his life. Because of the gender difference
between them, his mother Shirley was able to relate to
Eddie rather less ambivalently than she could to Margaret.
Society's premium on having a boy was reflected in how
Shirley felt towards this child. She was proud of having
produced a boy and this played out in subtle and overt ways.
As she said, she pampered him because he (unlike the girls)
would leave home one day and you couldn't cuddle a boy
when he was older, so she'd get her cuddling in now.
Because he was different from her she could imagine a
whole range of exciting adventures that would await him in
life and she spent time with him reading stories and
discussing affairs of the world. She was free from having to
hold back her desire to give unambiguously, for she need not
convey to him that he must restrain his wants and his desires.
When Eddie grew up he married a woman who loved him

deeply. They had a very good marriage and although circumstances meant that his work was less recognized than perhaps he might have wanted, he never suffered from the deep feelings of lack and unfulfilment that so plagued Margaret. His involvement with his wife was a constant source of strength to him.

We can hold on fiercely to idealized images of our parents because when we were little we needed them so much. They, especially our mothers, were our first contact with the world, the bridge to other relationships. We looked to them to make sense of our experiences, to explain, comfort, make all right, the hundreds of stimuli that we encountered. A child is apt to think that it is their fault if their needs go unmet or ignored by a parent. She or he feels that there is something lacking about her or him, or else the parent would be more attentive. It is a safer option for the child to preserve the parent as 'perfect' and to see itself as somehow naughty, silly, wrong, etc. than cope with the anxiety, anger and upset that is aroused when a child feels insufficiently emotionally supported. It is frightening to find fault with a parent early on. Even as we grow and need them less and expand our perceptions, our early images and the parallel denials run deep. As a child, Margaret had often stretched out her hand to her mother for help and when her mother was unresponsive Margaret took into herself the idea that she was perhaps asking too much. In this way her mother's image as a solid, reliable figure remained intact, while Margaret battled inside with the consequences of believing herself to be an over-needy little person.

What Margaret longed for from her husband Robert was a closeness and intimacy that she had never really experienced with her mother. In the early stages of their romance, when they were utterly fascinated and pleased by each other, their love for each other and their being loved rather took them out of themselves. This openness allowed them to feel very close and in Margaret's case it opened up her desire for warmth and contact. She felt as though a great weight had eased when she met Robert, that she no longer had to hold herself taut. She relaxed into the embracing hold of their relationship.

But as the relationship continued and Robert and Margaret were more assured of each other's presence, came to know each other better and weren't so utterly riveted by each other, other aspects of each of their personalities came to the fore and things began to change. Margaret felt dissatisfied with Robert; he was less concerned with her and she had many reactions to his withdrawal. She felt quite angry and depressed about losing what she felt had been such a precious contact between them. She held on to the memories of what had passed between them early on and longed to recapture the kind of love they had shared. But at the same time, dragging her down and more difficult to cope with, was the feeling of dread and disappointment that would come over her when she thought about how things would turn out. Margaret would come in contact with terribly upsetting feelings, like spasms of pain erupting, that things would always be this way, they wouldn't get much better, she couldn't or shouldn't expect them to, and that for some reason she was not going to have a happy marriage.

When Margaret was in touch with these kind of feelings she also 'knew', in a profound way, that it would be no different for her with anyone else. She lived on a seesaw, balanced between two confusing experiences she couldn't bring together. She saw Robert as a potential prince, as a wonderful man who (if only she could get him to, or if only he would spontaneously) could be more responsive, caring, stimulating and loving, and yet she saw herself as a woman full of needs but doomed not to have them fulfilled. *She didn't believe that Robert or anyone would really love her.*

Margaret was locked into a complicated and seemingly unsatisfying relationship. The disappointments in her earlier relationship with her mother which had been so well disguised were now reflected in a more open form in her relationship with Robert. Robert was idealized in similar ways to the idealization of her mother. There was an 'if only' quality to what Margaret felt . . . 'If only Robert would really

listen, if only Robert would really understand . . .' She held
on to the notion that Robert would be her prince. Because
she had never been allowed to be that dependent on her
mother, she still yearned to be dependent, to be attended
and cared for, but at the same time she didn't feel it was
possible, she didn't think Robert would be able to give her
what she wanted and needed. Inside she felt confirmed in
the knowledge that she would be pushed away once again.
So much of her life was spent in an emotional wasteland.
Bitterness and resentment grew to fill the void left by her
disappointment in love.

As we look with compassion at the stories of the other
women on these pages and we follow the threads that
connect each one's experience to another, we can't but help
see that many, many women juggle with similar kinds of
feelings of disappointment, anger and loss. We are forced to
the conclusion that there is something central to a girl's
upbringing that affects how she approaches an intimate
sexual relationship.

Sandra, forty, a mathematician, is married with three
children. For the first ten years of her marriage she and her
husband lived in the same house that her husband grew up
in. She took on the responsibility for looking after her
mother-in-law, who was somewhat infirm. For the last four
years, she has been having a passionate clandestine love
affair with Daniel, a graduate student in philosophy. Sandra
has been struggling with whether she should leave Leon, her
lawyer husband, and set up house for the kids and Daniel.
She feels she is living in a precarious situation and that her
deceit and the unhappy relationship with her husband will
have a bad effect on the children. She worries about whether
she could support herself and about how it would hurt the
children to lose daily contact with their father.

Sandra married a man who was still very attached to his
mother. He married quite late, at thirty-eight, because he
wasn't really able to make a commitment to another

woman, but Sandra did not see this when they were courting; she fell in love with his worldliness and experience and
felt that she would be able to learn so much from him, and be
stimulated by him. In reality Leon was not very available to
Sandra, and she gradually became aware of his deep attachment to his mother. When his mother died, Sandra hoped that
Leon would be able to move closer to her but sadly this did
not happen. Leon seemed a bit more subdued after the death
of his mother and Sandra was very protective of him, always
shooing the children away from the living room so that they
wouldn't disturb him. He could not talk much about the loss
of his mother and what it meant to him. He remained rather
remote and unreachable. Sandra was quite unhappy, for she
hoped that after the death they would be able to live as a
much closer family, able to determine their meal times and
what they would like to do, appropriate to a youngish
couple, now that they didn't need to defer to the wishes of
his mother. After a year or two had passed like this, Sandra
took up with her lover. She was aching to come alive
emotionally and was turned on by Daniel's energy and
sexual interest in her. She felt appreciated and loved, but she
did not feel the affair could possibly last because she was so
much older than Daniel and he would surely be 'better off'
with someone nearer his age. Sandra longed to be with
Daniel all the time, but she knew that there was, at the same
time, something quite important to her in the arrangement.
She had an inkling that life would not necessarily become
straightforwardly happier if she left Leon.

Sandra needed Leon, because she felt she needed a
husband, someone with whom she would have a daily
relationship, someone who would know her as she was,
someone who would provide her with a sense of continuity
and family. Sandra was dependent on Leon, but if we
examine the content of the dependency we can see that Leon
provided her with little more than a frame and a name to her
existence. She was a working wife and mother. He provided
her with a certain amount of economic security and
legitimacy in the eyes of others. But he wasn't available for

much else. For love and contact she had to go secretly to another man who was unable to provide the material security Leon gave her. Sandra yearned for the close relationship she had with Daniel to transfer to Leon, but her attachment to Leon was based in large measure on the fact of his unavailability. Sandra was involved with two men who were in their own ways providing less than she would have wanted. Daniel himself had a history of being involved with women who were involved with other men. When Sandra would discuss leaving Leon, Daniel would encourage her, and then drop out of sight for a couple of weeks. Daniel himself had never been able to sustain a relationship with women who were single, and so Sandra knew that being with him rested on there being real safeguards and boundaries in their relationship. Sandra was attracted to men who could only give in limited contexts. She could never bring all of herself to either of these men and feel really accepted. Sandra was restaging in her adult life an emotional play that she knew in her bones.

Her mother had been widowed when she was three and was depressed for many, many years. She had not been able to be much of a mother to Sandra because she was so wrapped up in her own distress and then later in a search for a new husband. When her mother remarried, Sandra was very happy. Her new father paid her lots of attention and was very interested in her development. Her mother, however, seemed to be jealous of their relationship and Sandra came to feel guilty if he spent a lot of time with her, so, as she grew up, she avoided her new father in an attempt to avoid hurting her mother.

The emotional drama we grow up in can be, even without our knowing it, like an imprint for life. It stays with us and shapes us and our expectations. What we observe in our parents' relationship to each other and to ourselves provides emotional signposts for what each individual feels entitled to get out of life. Unnurtured herself, Sandra saw her mother's unhappiness without a man and then observed her insecurity and jealousy with her new husband. In Sandra this was translated in the following ways: Sandra felt uneasy about having more than her mother; at the same time, she felt guilty that perhaps her mother had been deprived of meeting a man easily because of having a small child. The fact that her husband Leon's mother lived with them, then, was more than a passing coincidence. Caring for Leon's mother provided her with the opportunity to make reparations to her own mother for the deprivation she perceived in her life. She had so wanted her mother to be happy. The fact that Sandra was now involved with two men who were both unavailable was a replay of an emotional tableau she had known from her teenage years with her parents. Leon was now a stand-in for her rather depressed and repressive mother, as was his mother; Daniel was the loving stepfather whom she was required to love secretly. Sandra could tolerate a situation in which she was always negotiating stumbling blocks because she had absorbed the idea that she would never have much more to look forward to. Love and close relationships were not especially safe harbours; rather, she knew that the love that accompanied intimate relationships was shot through with disappointment, pain, depression, longing and guilt. There was a gap between what she so desperately wanted and what she felt she could have, and this gap was one she knew as well as she knew her own hand. It was so much a part of her emotional experience that she would have been lost without it. Sandra had grown up wanting something she could never name or put her finger on. She felt doomed to that wanting forever.

From the outside, none of these women's lives would seem to have been particularly troubled. But by shifting our focus ever so slightly we have seen that in important ways each of these women lived lives of private anguish, of disappointment and quiet despair. Helen sought closeness but couldn't handle it; Katie hid her dependency needs; Margaret stayed with someone who gave her very little; and Sandra couldn't allow herself to be dependent on anyone. Each woman had a substantial life separate from her relationship, and yet each woman felt she needed the relationship as the backdrop to her daily activities. Each woman wanted desperately to relate closely with a man. Each went on living in a relationship that had come to humiliate that ideal. Mingled with Margaret, Katie, Helen and Sandra's pain and upset was a partial recognition, a sense that this was all they would get, should hope for or deserved. They feared that they wanted too much. At the same time there was a rage, a rebellion, a fury, that in this, a most important aspect of a woman's life, so little true contact seemed possible.

We have to face a shocking and disturbing fact. The stories of Helen, Katie, Margaret and Sandra are stories of ordinary, educated, working women. There is nothing exceptional in their situations. They are almost too familiar to take notice of. We do begin to be startled however when we realize that their stories are duplicated by women in villages, cities and towns throughout the United Kingdom and America and that millions of women live lives of appalling emotional sterility and dissatisfaction. In our practice time and time again we hear women speak of their inability to accept and live with their own needs. Many women even deny that they have needs. Other women who do recognize their needs feel shame about having them.

Women have been brought up to look to men and intimate relationships to complete their lives. Women's psychologies have developed so that at a very deep level we feel that something is missing if we aren't in a close relationship. As women, when we look deep inside we may experience this feeling of missing in a general sense. Freud saw it in his women patients, and with his patriarchal spectacles he symbolically named this phenomenon for twentieth-century women as penis envy. As women psychotherapists, we understand this phenomenon in a different way. We hear women talk about how they don't like to be on their own, that they long to be really close to another human being, and yes, that there is something missing in their lives, a sense of a lack of completeness and wholeness. When we analyse these desires in terms of the individual history of each woman, and when we view her personal history in its social context, we see how dramatically social expectations shape our family relations, how children are raised and how parenting is conceived of, and then how these weave together to create the particular psychologies of women and men. We discover that women's inner feelings of lack relate to the construction in her of a psychology of femininity, a psychology that has denied her adequate satisfaction of the very basic need to be dependent.

Women, who on the face of it seem to be the dependent sex, are in reality involved in a cruel and unequal bargain that diminishes the quality of life for both men and women. Women are reared to provide for the dependency needs of others, to respond emotionally to their children, husbands, work mates, etc. Women develop emotional antennae that alert them to the needs of others. Women help those close to them process the disagreeable emotions that come up on a day-to-day basis. This process is so much part of all our experiences that we may not even notice it. Women, almost instinctively, pick up on the concerns of others — including other women's — and find one way or another to help the person come to terms with whatever is at hand. *What is missing in women's lives is that they have never had the consistent experience of this being done for them.* In fact, a woman's very sensitivity to this issue comes not just from the role-training she has received, but is itself a psychological reaction to her own rawness. Her neediness, her desire to be understood, to be taken into account, alerts her to such need in others. A woman's emotional world is strewn with neediness, both her own that she must so often repress, and that of others that she anticipates and responds to. Rarely does a woman say with confidence that her husband is able to anticipate and pick up the signals that she emits about her emotional state and what she might be needing. Part of what each of us looks for in an intimate relationship is just this kind of interchange, and so women suffer terribly when they don't find their partners adept in such ways. But, for this disappointment to be so profound and yet feel so inevitable as to be almost taken for granted at a subliminal level, it must spring from deeply buried emotional experiences. For if women were just brought up short by the disappointments in their relationships with men and that was all there was to it, they would either leave the specific relationship to look for another more satisfying one, going from man to man, or they would, as some women are now choosing to do, abandon the notion that men are able to satisfy them emotionally and look for loving intimate contact with women — or they would give up hope of enjoying any intimate relationship. But we know that not only Margaret, Katie, Sandra and Helen, but also many other women cling tenaciously to unsatisfying relationships, hoping they will change, fearing that they won't, wanting to leave but feeling unable to. Partly this is out of desperation, as we have seen, but this desperation needs to be integrated into the developmental picture of a women's psychology that we have sketched.

The woman's experience that there is something lacking, and her deep desire for attachment, are part of the same phenomenon. There are two aspects to the lacking or missing feelings that so many women report. On the one hand is the denial of the little girl's dependency needs and on the other are the psychological consequences of this denial. The denial — or perhaps, to describe it more accurately, an inconsistency in relating to a girl's dependency needs — produces in the girl feelings of lack of self-worth, of unentitlement and confusion. For, if a need is denied, one comes to feel all wrong about it and tries to do away with it. When this happens early on in life, the feeling that your needs are wrong translates into a feeling that you are wrong. The child feels that a part of her is wrong and unacceptable. In order to cope, she tries to push her needy part and the part of her that knows what she wants aside. She attempts to pursue things that others will find acceptable. She buries her dependent part and in the process loses a part of herself. This part, now in hiding, suffers by not being related to, so that the little girl is both alienated from an important aspect

of herself and further deprived of the nurturance she so
desperately wants.

This alienation is then followed by a psychological
dilemma. For, if as an infant one's dependency needs are not
met properly, then it is difficult to go to the next stage of
emotional development — the process of becoming your
own person. This developmental stage of separation and
individuation will be approached to some degree pre-
cociously, as an attempt to flee the painful state of unsatisfied dependency need, but at the same time with
residual, and hidden, resistance on the part of the child.

But, whatever route the child takes in trying to negotiate
its emotional growth, it will be hampered by being stuck, to
some extent, in that early stage of needing. These needs may
well be covered up, distorted, ignored or denied, or
displayed in a cloying, clinging way. However they emerge
they are an expression of the fact that the person's
dependency needs have *not* been met. Many people have
misunderstood this phenomenon and have observed rather
that a girl's attachment behaviour and a woman's clinginess
are a result of her dependent nature and now she is cosseted
and encouraged in early childhood. But the girl, later the
woman, suffers precisely for the opposite reason: because
her dependency needs were *not* sufficiently attended to
when they needed to have been. Unconsciously her longings,
and the fact that she never 'got enough', make it very hard
for her to separate psychologically from her mother, because deep inside her she still needs her so very much. If she
cannot have enough of her own mother, then she will bring
those kinds of needs into other relationships. She will search
for a mother in a friendship, in a marriage, always looking to
find the missing piece that will let her get close, take in the
nurturance she needs so that she can then move on and
become her own person. When women talk of there being
'something missing', they are trying to explain their mother's
missing nurturance that makes them feel less than whole.

We saw with Katie a common adaptation to the rejection
she felt of her infantile dependency. Katie developed a

strong, independent personality that was ready to take on difficult challenges. In a sense, Katie ran away from her dependency needs until she tripped over them in her relationship with Pete. She turned their denial into a virtue, relying only on herself for her most important needs, and thus she did not risk rejection. But Katie's adaptation meant that for many years she paid the terribly high price of not being involved and close to someone, of not having a soul mate. Her passage through the period of separation-individuation was marked by a brutal psychological divorce from her mother and an attempted severing of herself from the caretaker she needed so much. In this sense, Katie did not so much become her own separate person organically, but more as a result of the suppression of the little-girl part of her which had important needs that were not sufficiently responded to in infancy or afterwards. These needs were never met adequately, and it was their denial and repression that gave Katie the feeling that something was missing inside her. When she opened up to Pete, that little-girl part emerged and she felt whole within herself. She was reacquainted with a part of her that had been buried and rejected for a long time. In a sense she was getting back what she was missing, a core part of her personality. The difficulty came because unknowingly she invested the change in her working situation with all the meaning of attempting to redo a process that had been so painful to her thirty-eight years before. She was trying, now that she felt more whole, to go out on her own, with a sense of solidity, eagerness and genuine confidence. She was struggling to be independent from a base of rich and loving support rather than as a flight from a situation in which she wasn't getting her needs met. Her previous 'independent' stance in reality actually embodied a defence against her being in a stage of acknowledged but unmet dependency. In leaving her job she had been trying to rewrite history.

Katie, and the other women we have met, turned to men to meet needs that mothers seemed unable to meet for them. What were these needs that mothers didn't meet?

What was the texture of the early relationship between these mothers and daughters? What do so many daughters feel was missing? Why do so many women feel so disappointed? And what does it tell us about women's lives, women's expectations and the effects of women being second class?

In every case we have analysed in our practice, in workshops, in one-to-one therapy, with women of all ages who were raised mainly by their mothers, we have observed similar features in the mother-daughter relationship. Women who themselves are mothers or about to become mothers come to therapy and tell of their experiences with *their* mothers. Women who come to talk about their relationships with men, husbands and fathers, find themselves speaking of the bittersweet emotions in their relationships with their mothers; they are bursting to come to grips with this most powerful and fundamental first relationship.

Without exception, all of these women share a terribly confusing experience. They feel tied to their mothers and 'taken over' by them. They experience mother as interfering, that she expects unreasonable things and is controlling. At the same time they feel pushed away (denied), not terribly well understood and not seen for who they are. They feel a tug of war between their needs and the needs of their mother. We have heard this expressed so frequently that we have begun to call this an effect of the push-pull dynamic in the mother-daughter relationship. Mothers express enormous love and care for their daughters but this love is tinged with ambivalence that comes from the mother's inner feelings about herself, her femininity, and how she feels consciously and unconsciously about having a daughter. Mothers relate to their daughters in this fashion because they were similarly related to by their mothers. Inside each mother lives a repressed little girl who is still yearning for acceptance and love. Katie's mother's jealousy of what she was giving her daughter was unusual in that she was aware of these rather unpleasant feelings. Mothers are bound to have complicated feelings about nurturing their daughters for various reasons.

Because of their social position and the demands that go with it, mothers, who are themselves second-class citizens, are in the unenviable situation of having to raise their daughters to step into their shoes. In other words, it is the job of those who are themselves in a subordinate position to prepare the next generation of girls to take their place. This is cruel and ironic, for in mothering daughters women are in an almost impossible position. While they want to and do give emotionally, they must prepare their daughters for a life in which the daughters will not be able to expect entirely equal rights. They need to help their daughters take up the feminine role and pitch their expectations at an appropriate level. Obviously this is not carried out in either a particularly conscious way, or even in the bald sense that we have just stated it. Mothering is a complex process that is much richer than any analysis of it could possibly convey. But mothering is also a social process, which is to say that it takes place under particular conditions, with certain demands and pressures that are shaped by larger forces that affect the very intimacy of the one-to-one mother-child relationship.

One of the unwritten social practices in which we all share complicity, to one extent or another, is in the unequal exchange of women's and men's dependency needs. The fact that women are raised to provide nurturance, care and attention, to have others depend on them emotionally, and that boys are not, acts as a pressure in the mother-daughter relationship in four particular ways.

First, mothers need to prepare their daughters to become givers. A woman's self-esteem suffers if she doesn't feel herself to be a 'good giver'. Consciously and unconsciously then, mothers encourage and reinforce a daughter's moves to be caring, to develop her emotional radar, to be responsive. Mother tells her daughter not to be selfish but generous, to pay attention to others' needs, to extend a hand (ultimately a lap), an invisible net of support.

Second, more than likely, mother is not receiving the kind

of nurturance she wants in her marriage and so her daughter sees that mother and father's relationship is unequal. Mother may complain to her husband or she may comply. She may or may not convey her feelings directly to her daughter. A daughter will, however, pick up the traces of mother's emotional dissatisfaction. She takes in the idea that her mother, whose gender she shares, and therefore like whom she will become, wants things from her father that she doesn't get. Her mother, a grown woman, is somewhat unsatisfied.

Third, because she is to some extent needy herself, the mother may look to her daughter for the emotional contact that is missing elsewhere in her life. In teaching her daughter how to give to others, she may, without even realizing it, offer herself as a candidate, and their relationship may become burdened by needs that she doesn't have satisfied elsewhere.

Fourth, the mother herself is a daughter, and the daughter of a daughter. Her early development has been marked by similar emotional shaping to that her daughter is experiencing. Her mother had to teach her how to become a woman, and to hold back from wanting too much. These struggles are unconsciously revived when she relates to her own daughter. She feels the loss of her own mother's nurturance and may hope that her daughter will make up for it somehow.

For these reasons, mothering a daughter is fraught with particular strains. A mother may find it hard to respond without ambivalence. At times she can spontaneously love, give, listen, comfort, reassure and encourage her daughter. At other times, she will withdraw, restrain, criticize and judge. The attitudes that accompany these actions may well be unconscious; a mother herself may be surprised at her inconsistent behaviour towards her daughter. Many women speak of the shock they feel when they hear themselves sounding just like their own mothers when they are talking to their daughters. For example, Margaret would often hear herself scolding her own daughter — 'don't get upset' — as though her mother was speaking her lines. A woman may feel herself to be a 'loving' mother and be brought up short when she stumbles on the ways in which she curtails her daughter emotionally. These emotional factors entwine with the requirements of the role she is introducing her daughter to. The daughter becomes a potential nurturing and dependable person for mother, at the same time as she goes through a childhood with feelings of loss and incompleteness herself.

Because a woman may not have received enough nurturance in her life, which is to say that she may never have felt someone was really there for her, she may not have been able to feel a secure sense of self. She will be constantly looking for the person, the close relationship, which will give her security and fill up the emptiness. Sadly, men whom she turns to are not likely to have developed nurturing skills. Restricted in the public world to one degree or another, and disappointed in her close relationship, a woman will often have a child or children to fill the void and to have someone with whom she is in a dependent relationship. A child can be someone in her life to whom she is undeniably attached. A woman can give to her child and obtain a certain kind of satisfaction when she projects herself into her child's shoes and then absorbs what she imagines the child is experiencing.

The reader may well feel suffocated by the concentration on the mother-daughter relationship in these pages. They may wonder where father is and how he influences a girl's developing psychology and her adult relationship with men. For most of us, father was not very much present in the crucial period of infantile dependency when our personalities began to form. Few of us spent more than a half-hour or so with our father at each end of the working day. For most of the week he was absent and it was mother who gave to us and to whom we turned when we wanted something. Father lives on the edge of the little girl's world. He is always coming and going. His presence and absence affects the emotional atmosphere. When he is around he receives mother's attention; when he leaves that attention returns

to us. Fathers relate in a staccato fashion to their daughters
— as do mothers, in a completely different way. Fathers can
feel awkward handling children until they are strong enough
to rough and tumble. They may not know how to comfort a
baby's distress and, without even realizing it, pass a crying
baby back to its mother's arms. From the little girl's point of
view, Daddy is a mystery, a powerful figure who is always
leaving. She has no power to keep him there or to get the
attention she wants from him. He is experienced as separate
and different and outside her immediate world. When, as a
toddler, she is separating from mother, father's position
outside the orbit attracts her. She may go to him to get what
she still needs so much, or she may approach him having
hidden her needy part. But, however she approaches him,
his availability will be restricted by the demands of his social
role. She will perceive that she cannot and should not
expect too much of his time. She comes to feel somewhat
powerless in her inability to make her father be there for her.
Her relationship with him does not fill in the missing contact,
for it too is marked by inconsistency. Father responds to her
cuteness and charm, to her attempts to please him and
engage him. He does not rescue her from the difficult
aspects of her relationship with mother. He does not want to
see her needy and wanting part. He does not offer her a real
alternative. Her relationship with him is constricted in its
own ways. It will affect all her future relationships with men.

   Women live with painful feelings of deprivation; with
longings for care, love, acceptance and emotional contact.
Each woman in her individual life and relationships searches
to fill up the emptiness inside and to make peace with this
powerful theme of dependency and attachment.

3

The Great Taboo: Men's Dependency

One hears very little about the topic of men and dependency. Somehow, by definition, men are supposed not to be dependent. The very notion of masculinity excludes dependence. Men are seen to be the providers, the breadwinners, the protectors of women and children, strong people with little emotional need upon whom the family can lean. Women and children are supposed to depend on men. Men are not supposed to show their vulnerability for it implies weakness — a dreaded characteristic in a man. A man's vulnerability shatters a myth. All of a sudden he is seen to have fears and insecurities and still to need reassurance and comfort.

Women like both aspects of men's personalities. Women like men's confidence in themselves and competence in the world. There is a sense of excitement in the difference between his 'world', his way of being, his maleness and her own experience as a woman. Women collude in the perpetuation of the myth of the strong man, for if there is a strong man the woman can imagine that she is safe, that she is being cared for and looked after. Women are also drawn to men's openness. Women talk about falling in love with a man and getting closer to him *because* he has exposed his vulnerable side. Showing himself, he 'gives' her something. He has let her have a peek behind the mask of masculinity. She feels drawn to the person 'inside'. Maybe he's not so different, maybe he's not so scary, maybe he's not so big, maybe he can be playful, maybe he can be a friend, a mate.

A man may feel that he must woo a woman with his masculinity. When he first meets a woman he feels under

some pressure to perform with confidence and assertive-
ness. He 'knows' that this is what women are supposed to be
attracted to, and he wants to be successful in his love affairs.
But at the same time, men are eager to have a woman with
whom they can share another part of themselves. It may
only be with a woman that a man's emotional vulnerability
emerges. It is taboo for men to expose that aspect of their
personalities to each other for it signifies emotionality and
femininity. In friendships with other men a man may feel
starved of intimate emotional contact. It is permitted
somewhat for a man to be engaged emotionally with
another man in an unequal relationship. That is, men can
have emotional exchange as father/son, big brother/little
brother.

Women *and* men suffer within a patriarchal culture. From
birth both sexes are restricted in many areas of expression.
For the boy, growing up to be a man means being
able to act in the world. There are many benefits to being
regarded as someone of substance, as someone with some
degree of power. But there is a severe psychological price
that boys pay for their ticket into patriarchy. A boy must
dissociate himself from the world of his mother — his first
world, the world of the home, the world of women. The boy
must identify with his father, who, to some extent, is a
stranger compared to the familiar feel and smell of mother.
The boy must be like his father and go into the world. But
here a psychological problem presents itself, for in the first
year of life the infant boy is still psychologically merged
with his mother, has taken aspects of her personality into
himself in the developing of his own personality. His mother
is inside him; she is a part of him. He develops through the
psychological phase of separation-individuation and begins
to experience his separateness from his mother and his own
boundaries. Simultaneously he is confronting gender awareness, which for the little boy may be an equally difficult
psychological task. As he comes to realize that he is different
from his mother, he begins to identify consciously with his
father because of their shared gender. His mother and father

are different. He is like his father. He is not like his mother.
Not only is he a separate person from his mother but he is
also a different person in a central way. At the point at
which (as early as age two) he begins to identify himself as
a boy, he must keep his mother's femininity out. He must
begin to develop a sense of himself as different from her. As
the boy grows this separateness becomes established. He is a
boy; he plays with boys' toys; he won't play with dolls and
dishes; he won't wear aprons; he plays with tools and guns;
he plays 'going out to work' instead of house; he wants to be
like daddy. *Being like daddy becomes translated into a
denial of the ways in which he is like mother and a denial of
the fact that she is already a part of him.*

He must act in male ways — he must not cry; he must try
to win, to come in first, to succeed. His sense of himself
comes to depend on his achievements, his mastery. His self-
confidence rests on his competence with the games he plays,
life at school, etc. He is encouraged to compete. He is
encouraged to win at all costs. He feels terrible if he loses at a
game; it upsets something inside, it shakes his confidence.

His mother is there encouraging him on. She is a part of his
experience as he relies on her support and love. The mother,
caught in the web of patriarchal parenting, cooperates in the
creation of a split in her son's personality. She relates to her
son with all of her own unconscious beliefs and assumptions
about who boys and men are and can be in the world.
Unconsciously her son's gender affects the way she relates to
him. She is proud to have produced a son, a little prince,
while she feels resentful of the life opportunities that he
will have, because he is a boy, that were denied her. She
encourages her son to be a man. In so doing the mother
unwittingly colludes in her son's psychological negation of
her. Who he is rests on his denial of what he has taken in from
her, of how much he is 'like' her. Men's psychology contains
a split — the part that is seen in the world, acts in appropriate
male ways; and the part that is buried deep in the unconscious in the earliest infantile memories, of emotional,
physical, psychological merger with his mother.

In an intimate relationship with a woman this hidden part of the man's personality gets touched. In connecting closely once again with a woman, a man may let down some of his defences. But these particular defences are a central feature of men's psychology — he unconsciously feels he needs them in order to carry on in the world, in order to continue to know himself. These defences developed early in life and they are a part of his psychic structure. Letting down these defences, for many men, seems an impossibility.

Paradoxically, however, although men must deny aspects of mother that are inside, they can continue to rely on mother's support and care. A boy can feel secure in having his mother look after him, clothe him, prepare his meals, clean up after him, encourage him, nurture him. *More importantly, boys can look forward to this in later life from another woman, his wife, who will replace mother.* As we have illustrated in Chapter 2, this experience is not symmetrical for the girl.

We now begin to get a glimmer of the true picture of men and dependency. For although, like women's, men's dependency needs are hidden, in fact men's dependency needs are more continually met. Internally as well as externally, there is a camouflaging process taking place. The internal camouflage is the denial of mother — a denial of men's original dependency on a woman to survive. This internal camouflage is aided by the psychological defences which aim to maintain the masculine sense of self. The external camouflage is the ideology which states that women are dependent, weak and helpless whilst men are independent, strong and autonomous. Here there is a camouflaging of adult men's continued dependency on women emotionally, sexually and physically.[1]

1. This is one of the critical mistakes Colette Dowling makes in her book *The Cinderella Complex*. Ms. Dowling never looks at the way men's dependency needs are catered to and more regularly satisfied than are women's, thereby enabling men to go out into the world and be 'independent' and successful. They do that with the security of a home base.

Men depend on women in material ways as well as
emotional ones. How often do we hear women say that
they hope their husband dies first because their husband
wouldn't be able to survive without them? That they won't
be able to boil an egg or know where anything in the house is
without first asking the wife? The women's liberation
movement has opened the door of the household and
exposed the whole issue of domestic labour. But so far
feminists have looked at only one aspect of that labour.
We've called attention to the unjust power relations which
have women doing all the unpaid housework, which is then
undervalued. We've seen male privilege as men sit back with
their slippers on watching the television as the wife endlessly
cleans and cooks, etc. What we have not yet analysed about
that situation is the way in which men continue to be
dependent, like boys with mothers who look after them
and cater to their physical needs. Especially today, when
more and more women are either forced or are choosing
to work outside the home, the assymetry cries out. Men
continue to have a 'mother'; women do not. From boyhood
to manhood, although men may make enormous strides
outside the home, in the domestic sphere their lives remain
constant. Boys have their food bought and cooked; boys
have their clothes laundered and ironed; boys have their
homes attended to, cleaned; boys have mother's shoulder to
cry on; boys have mother's encouragement about who they
can be in the world. In an unchallenged patriarchal household, men have their food bought and cooked; men have
their homes attended to, cleaned; men have their wives'
shoulders to cry on; men have their wives' encouragement
about their success in the world. There is a continuity in
boys' early experience of dependency which extends on into
adolescence and manhood. These examples of dependency
are examples of material and physical survival. But they
have their emotional complement. The mother is always
there. The person who was raised to become a mother, a
nurturer and emotional caretaker of others, is there for him.
Boys can live with the expectation of continued maternal

nurturance, first from mother and later from a wife. At the
same time as men acquire power in the outside world — by
being born male in a patriarchal culture — they continue to
be looked after (as children are) at home.

As we have seen, developmental psychologists have
observed that, in order to achieve successful autonomy,
separation and a secure sense of self, the toddler must have a
secure 'home base'. That is, the child must feel, as he or
she steps out into the world and away from its mother, that
its mother will not disappear; that she will be there as the
anchor, the safety net of love and encouragement. With this
security the child can expand its world and come to feel the
world is a safe place.

In looking at little boys' and later men's experience we
find some resonance with 'healthy' developmental theory.
For although a boy has the difficult task of separating from
his mother psychologically, identifying with his father and
developing a sense of himself that is different from his
mother, at the same time the boy does not lose his mother.
He does not have to give her up or, more importantly, he
does not have to give up the expectation of maternal
nurturance, or indeed the nurture itself. They have the
psychological task of separation (as do girls, who must
separate from the same-gendered person, making it to our
minds even more difficult), but they do not have to let go
emotionally of their need for a woman to continue to care
for and look after them.

Revealing men's dependency needs threatens a deeply
held inner conception of the way things are for both men
and women. Recognizing a man's need for a woman brings
up for all of us the power of women. In our society, where
by and large women raise children, women are very
powerful people. In our memory we hold an image of a
big person who held, fed and protected us. So although
women's nurturing and 'mothering' abilities are so thoroughly undervalued in general, if we look closely we see
that for men and women alike a woman was an extremely
powerful person in their lives. If we accept that men are

in fact dependent on women emotionally we need to go a step further and look more closely at men's attachment to women.

Frank is a solicitor for a law centre. He is thirty-four years old and has never been married. He has been involved in various relationships with women since he was seventeen. The relationships have lasted from several dates to a couple of two- to three-year relationships. There was a pattern in how the important, long-term relationships ended. With several of the women Frank dated he stopped because he wasn't interested enough. In his three-year relationship with Joan things started really well, they both were in love and excited about being together and then, gradually, difficulties began. They began to have regular fights — some of which were resolved well, but others left a residue of 'bad' feelings which took away from the initial joyful ones of love. Frank began to feel that Joan didn't understand that he had been under a lot of pressure at university and that he had to devote time and attention to his work. Joan complained that he didn't think of her, that he didn't 'court' her anymore and that he treated her like a piece of the furniture. He felt furious with her for her complaints and 'nagging', and began to feel that she was only an additional pressure in his life; making him feel bad, angry and taking up too much of his energy which he needed for his career. They decided to end it.

After several years of dating, Frank met Mindy. He was very attracted to her both physically and intellectually. Mindy was a social worker committed to things that he was committed to — things which led him to work for the law centre. Frank felt more mature, felt that he had settled into his profession, that his experiences with women had been good for him at the time. Now at thirty-two Frank was optimistic about developing a committed relationship with Mindy. He knew that he wanted a family and it seemed that maybe he should start to think about this more seriously. For the first year the relationship progressed almost effortlessly.

Frank was in love, excited and filled with happiness that here was a woman he felt he could really love. Frank found himself thinking about Mindy throughout each day and eagerly awaited the evenings when they would be together. He took Mindy to his favourite restaurants, bought good bottles of wine for their evenings in. They decided to live together. Frank was happy. He felt that Mindy, too, was happy and Frank felt confident that she loved him. Frank felt that he now had everything he dreamed of — his law work and a woman he loved who loved him.

Two years later Frank and Mindy came to us for counselling because they were on the verge of splitting up. Why? Mindy felt that Frank was always absorbed in his work and that he no longer understood her or knew what was going on in her life. She felt he no longer gave to her or loved her. Frank did not understand this at all. He knew that he still loved and wanted Mindy and, although he agreed that they had become more distant, he did not feel there was a loss of love. It wasn't until Mindy told him that she was thinking of leaving that he became fully aware of how serious the situation was. At first he blamed Mindy and thought that it was really because she was not satisfied by *her* work and that she was looking to their relationship for too much in her life. He thought this was 'neurotic' on her part. But deep inside Frank felt frightened because this seemed to be a repeat of his relationship with Joan. He was scared that there was something wrong in the way he behaved in a relationship. Mindy seemed to say so many of the things that Joan had said. Mindy described how she felt ignored by Frank; that the time spent at home more frequently was spent with Frank looking over his work, preparing briefs, etc., and that when Frank wanted to relax he put on the television, watched sports, read the newspaper. During the counselling Frank said that he didn't understand Mindy's complaints; they were so elusive he really didn't know what she wanted from him.

Frank and Mindy's experience has been echoed by many couples. Women complain of men taking them for granted;

of men not 'knowing' them deeply or not understanding them sufficiently. Men, meanwhile, often feel bewildered by this and don't really understand what it is the woman is talking about. It feels like she's just complaining again, 'bitching', nagging'. 'What *do* women want?' If we unravel the intricacies of Frank's attachment to Mindy we see one example of how men's psychology and their dependency come into play in relationships with women. At the beginning of the relationship Frank wanted Mindy; he was attracted to her personality and looks and he had the desire to be closer to her. While they were going out together, Frank gave a lot of himself. He was extremely interested in listening to Mindy, in hearing about her work, her personal history, the way she saw the world, etc. He was building an emotional attachment to her and hoping that she would reciprocate his feelings. He wanted Mindy to desire him as much as he desired her. As their relationship developed Frank continued to appreciate Mindy. He was happy to be going home to her, looking forward to sharing stories of the day each had had. Frank felt that Mindy understood him and cared tenderly for him. He allowed himself to be vulnerable with her; to tell her of his fears and worries about his work, about himself. He felt accepted by Mindy and her love provided him with good feelings about himself which he took with him out the door each morning. He needed and loved Mindy. He felt close to her and open. What was the problem? Because their relationship had such a strong foundation and because Frank felt so secure in his home life, he was, in fact, taking Mindy for granted. He was unaware of his dependency needs because he was satisfied. Frank unconsciously felt that he could depend on Mindy being there with him always. His attachment to her resonated at a psychological level with what he had always been raised to expect: a woman to love him and be with him. He was, in fact, content and in love. That is why Mindy's statement of feeling he didn't love her seemed ludicrous to him. Of course he loved her. As we have seen in Chapter 2, girls, because they must give up maternal nurturance, have in their psychology the anticipated loss of a nurturing person. Just as a young boy feels mother is there, regardless of how much he gives back to her, so too did Frank come to assume that Mindy would be there no matter what. In the counselling Frank realized that on an emotional level he did stop 'courting' Mindy; that he didn't listen to and give her the emotional attentiveness and care that he had at the beginning of their relationship. He realized that it actually had to be a conscious process for him to relate intimately because left to his own unconscious motivations he would not struggle to relate emotionally. He saw where he had to push himself to overcome his own social-ization to a male emotional role. He had to learn how to give and how to be emotionally nurturing to another person.

Rubin is thirty-six years old. He feels that his relationships with women are repeated disasters. For some reason, unbeknownst to him, Rubin falls in love with women who are unavailable. He doesn't know how he does it, but inevitably he becomes attracted to women who are married or involved with someone else. Rubin's friends have intro-duced him to single women but none have ever really engaged him. It's as if the spark is missing. Rubin ex-periences time and time again situations, at work, at parties and social gatherings, where he becomes attracted to a woman who is with another man. Rubin is a lab technician and several times he met women with whom he liked working at the lab. There was Anne who worked on the fourth floor. Rubin noticed her around and finally invited her to lunch. She accepted and Rubin found himself unable to think about anything but Anne for the days before the lunch date. It was a big disappointment when Anne told him that she lived with Jack. Then there was Alison. For months Rubin was aware of Alison in the radiology lab. Every time something had to be delivered from his department to her lab, he leaped at the chance to make the delivery so that he could see Alison. She seemed very friendly to him. Rubin

thought about her in fantasies before drifting off to sleep. He
imagined he and Alison together and in love. Finally after
several months Rubin overcame his anxiety and asked
Alison if she'd like to go out with him. She accepted. It
turned out that Alison had recently broken up with someone.
She was still upset about the ending of that relationship.
Rubin felt sympathetic and listened to Alison and talked
with her about her old boyfriend. After a month of dating,
Alison told Rubin that she was going back to him. She was
very sorry but couldn't help it; she still loved him. Rubin
was distraught. He felt he would never have a woman
he wanted. He felt he had failed again.

Rubin's experience illustrates another aspect of men's
dependency problems. Rubin constantly finds himself in a
familiar drama. The cast of characters are a woman, a man
whom the woman is somewhat attached to, and Rubin.
Rubin is always psychologically on the line; that is to say
there is a goal which is extremely difficult to achieve because
there are significant blocks in the way, and Rubin's sense of
adequacy and sense of self is connected to whether or not he
can reach his goal. What is this drama that Rubin and so
many men play out again and again? Let's first look at it
historically and analytically. As an infant the boy 'has' his
mother. They are the couple. As the boy gets a bit older he
comes to see that, in fact, mother is also attached to another
man. This is psychologically jolting for the little boy who has
to learn to negotiate this new triangle. He has complicated
feelings about father. He sees the powerful position father
maintains vis-à-vis mother. The boy is encouraged to identify with his father, to form a bond, an alliance based on their
shared gender. He looks forward to being like father and
hopes one day to have 'a girl just like the girl that married
dear old dad'. In Rubin's case his mother was, in fact, a
distant person. She found it difficult to show love openly to
her children; she was withdrawn emotionally. This affected
Rubin and his sister differently. For Rubin was able to
'escape' his early merger with mother by turning towards
father, who was, in fact, more emotionally accessible, and

identifying with him.[2] Secondly, Rubin could move away
from the pain of his early feelings of deprivation by looking
ahead to a future in which he could have a woman love him
'better'. It is as if Rubin lives with a piece of unfinished
business unconsciously all the time. He needs to feel loved,
he needs to be shown that he is worthy. He tells himself that
the reason he doesn't have this is because there is another
man who is getting the love. He struggles painfully time and
again to win the love of a woman. The test is out of
proportion to 'normal' loving — available women, women
who like him immediately, won't do. They can't repair the
damage inside. They can't fit the role which will eventually
re-write the drama with a good ending. If a woman is
available and interested in Rubin there is no fire, no sparks,
no challenge. Unconsciously he tries to be the winner in the
triangle so that he can undo those painful experiences of
rejection. But alas, he finds the rejection repeated again and
again, only to confirm what he feels and fears inside; that he
will not be loved and desired by a woman, that he will feel
painfully alone and outside. His dependency needs were not
satisfied early on in life and he is hungry and feels unworthy.

For other men, the unavailable woman may signify
something else. Many men feel frightened of an intimate
involvement with a woman, feel that their dependency is
potentially too great or feel that they must maintain their
separateness because their confidence is shaky, so the
unavailability of a woman provides a protection, a barrier.
He can 'go after' her, fantasize about her, feel sexual feelings
in relation to her, feel love for her — at a distance. There are
different reasons why a man may feel he needs a barrier
between himself and a woman. He may feel that women are
controlling and involvement with a woman means giving up
an inner sense of freedom. He is attracted to women and
pursues them with great enthusiasm, but intimacy and

2.   This was not the same for Rubin's sister, whose identity was caught in
      the merger with mother first, and second, she could not have the ex-
      pectation of a future 'better' mothering experience.

commitment make him feel trapped. He must maintain his
independence in order to maintain his sense of self. These
men may have experienced their mothers as holding on to
them, clinging to them, needing them too much. They had to
break free and that was a difficult struggle (maybe they
haven't yet succeeded with their mothers) and so involvement with a woman seems dangerous. Popular culture feeds
that particular image with expressions such as 'she hooked
him', 'she caught him', and the like. We hold images of free
animals being roped into domesticity.

Some men manage to negotiate this fear by half measures.
Many men can be in a committed relationship and enjoy the
intimacy and security such a relationship can provide, but
must at the same time have affairs. Some men find that they
won't have an affair, but find themselves looking at and
attracted to other women in a rather obsessional way. Men
may look to these other women in order to maintain a sense
of autonomy — of life outside the couple — of freedom.
There is also something exciting about the newness of the
other woman, a sense of not yet 'possessing' this 'object'; of
knowing one's wife very well and of feeling secure in
'having' her and so the excitement of 'getting' her is gone.
This sense of going after something, conquering it, master-
ing it, possessing it, establishing control, is all part and parcel
of a boy's socialization to the male role. Whereas women
often seek confidence and security *within* the couple and
from attachment to their partner, men may need to maintain
and secure a sense of themselves from outside.

The phenomenon of 'don't disturb daddy' is familiar to
many of us. Men's boundaries are sensed and respected by
others. A man can create a separate enclave even within his
own home. We see this most easily with dad reading the
newspaper or watching news and sports on television; dad
'working' on something either brought home from outside or
a household repair of some sort; dad taking a nap and
everyone being instructed by mother to tip-toe around and
not disturb him. There is an acceptance that men need some
privacy and that entering those invisible boundaries is

serious business with serious consequences for the intruder. This rarely is the same with women. (Recently women have been struggling to be taken seriously when they are work-ing: they are busy and not to be disturbed.) Children tend to go to mother for all sorts of things and don't give a second thought to 'disturbing' her when she's cooking, cleaning, reading, watching TV etc. Men determine and are more in control of their availability.

Alan and Marjorie are both writers and work at home. Alan has had two novels published. Marjorie has had less public recognition for her writing although she has published several magazine articles and short stories. They are both in their early thirties and do not have children. They have separate rooms in which they work. Alan begins by 9 a.m. and absorbs himself quite thoroughly in his writing. He comes out of the room for an occasional cup of coffee, a sandwich, a short break. Sometimes he looks in on Marjorie at her work, says hello, chats for a few minutes. Marjorie finds herself responding and taking short breaks when Alan does. Her concentration is easily broken. It's as if she's always ready to relate if she is made aware of Alan's presence. She cannot keep him out of her awareness. On the other hand, Marjorie looks in on Alan when she takes a walk from the desk and sees that he is absorbed and working and usually either of two things happens. Marjorie may not say anything to him for fear of disturbing and angering him, or if she asks if he wants a cup of coffee his response often is to acknowledge a yes or no and remain concentrated in his work. Even if Marjorie brings the coffee to him, he nods or says thanks and carries on. The presence of another person does not have the same effect on Alan as on Marjorie. When he is within his own world and boundaries, he can stay there; the coming and going of Marjorie does not disturb his equilibrium.

Yet, the consequences of being raised a boy are equally severe but in a different way. First of all we suggest that a man's separateness, and therefore his ability to feel a person in his own right, rests on a bizarre reversal of identification and power. He realizes that he is not like his mother (till then the most powerful figure in his life) and in seeing himself as different from her, he must deny the power she has. Social realities of men's power mean that the boy sees his father's power at the same time as he is coming to identify with him. There is an intricate process whereby the social laws of patriarchy, the position of the mother and the developmental stage of psychological separation and gender identification weave together, and unbeknownst to him the boy is caught in the web of patriarchal power relations and he must find his place. We suggest that in his unconscious there remains a memory of mother's power and also a memory of his denial of that power and of his own internal conversion of those power relations. Therefore, buried in the unconscious is also a fear as well as admiration for women.

Men's ability to be 'separate', then, rests on a firm set of defences constructed to maintain a sense of himself as male, as other. These strong defences and boundaries in some sense also represent a fragility in his psychology — it is unintegrated. In other words, there is both a 'healthy' sense of 'keeping people out', of autonomy, as well as a defensive position of keeping people out so that they don't come too close, don't get inside, don't discover....

Growing up a boy and developing into a man in patriarchal society causes splits in men's psychology which have quite crippling effects for mature emotional exchange in adult relationships. Men often feel uncomfortable in situations in which there is open emotional intercourse. A man may feel embarrassed, nervous, awkward at the outward display of emotionality or uncomfortable about what is expected of him. He may retreat into his other world, the world of work. In times of emotional crisis the job of comforting, sympathizing or dealing with the upset is most often turned over to women to handle. Even when it is a member of the man's family who is in the distressing situation it is the wife who deals with the event. Men look to women to provide the

social grease. What is remarkable is the way in which on one
level this is all invisible — that is, men's dependency on
women — while at the same time it is blatantly apparent. We
speak of the classic hostess who enables everyone to feel at
ease, or the wife who calls her mother-in-law, sisters-in-law,
etc., and maintains the family nexus. We say 'what would he
do without her', but we fail to see this as an aspect of men's
dependency on women.

Being raised as a boy in our society hampers men in their
emotional relationships. Responding to another's emotional
needs, giving nurture, is a potential which all human beings
possess. But this potential, just like so many others, must be
developed. It is not formed at birth, it is not natural and
inevitable because of one's biology as male or female. In our
culture nurturing becomes woven with gender and femininity. 'Mothering' is something girls are continually given
the opportunity to develop in themselves. Girls are given
dolls to practise on, girls are given tea sets in order to
rehearse feeding and serving others, girls are continually
told to 'be nice', which for a girl means not fighting, letting
others have their way, being selfless. We know that this
training in a rigid sex-role society is extremely oppressive to
girls, but there is no doubt that at the same time girls are
developing a part of themselves, a human potential of
nurturing and giving and thinking about others. Boys are
discouraged from developing that part of themselves. In the
same way that girls' outward, active, achieving, daring and
energetic aspects of their personalities are hampered and
restrained, so on the other side of the coin are boys'
emotional, caring, gentle, nurturing, relational aspects of
their personalities denied growth and development. Boys
who show interest in playing with dolls, or even playing with
girls for that matter, are considered 'sissies' — a curse of
being like a girl — so deep are the taboos against boys'
continued identification with mother and femininity. Boys
receive direct prohibitions about developing nurturant
characteristics. Perhaps more significantly in terms of men's
psychology, not only is that aspect of mother which the boy

embodies not fostered and developed, it is repressed in the
unconscious where it takes on a much deeper and scarier
meaning. 'When my wife had our first child I felt very afraid
to hold the baby. It wasn't that I was afraid I'd drop her or
anything, it was more that I felt nervous, ashamed. I noticed
that when I was alone in the baby's room I felt relaxed in
holding her. In fact I loved it. But as soon as someone else
came into the room or if we were in a situation where there
were other people I just felt too uncomfortable. I would
want my wife to hold her. One afternoon we had my brother
and his wife and their kids over and another couple who are
friends of ours. We all were sitting in the living room and my
wife was making something in the kitchen. Jessie (the baby)
was crawling on the floor and started to cry. I went to pick
her up to comfort her and I saw my brother watching me.
Suddenly I felt overwhelming anxiety. I managed not to
show it but later that night I told my wife about it. As we
talked I suddenly had the memory of playing house with my
next-door neighbour. I was about six years old. There were
two girls living next door and the three of us were playing
with dolls, dressing them, giving them bottles and things like
that. We heard laughing outside and when I looked up there
was my brother who was three years older than me and a
bunch of his friends laughing and pointing and calling me sis-
sie and saying Ralph plays with dolls, Ralph plays with dolls,
again and again. I wanted to run away and hide forever.'

Boyhood is filled with repeated messages that being a boy
means *not* being like a girl. Boys' friendships develop
within an atmosphere of boys *doing* things together; moving, being active, thinking about how things work, watching
men compete in sports, etc. Friendship with other boys is
crucially important and having a good friend, someone to
play with, rely on, is very much needed. But by adolescence
we already see where male friends have difficulty in giving
each other what they need. Feelings of insecurity, anxiety,
fear which get aroused during adolescence when the young
man is experiencing his sexuality and his new interest in girls
are rampant and yet talking about feelings (especially ones

with 'negative' connotations implying weakness) is some-thing boys are ill-prepared to do. In adolescence we see the split in men's psychology widen even more as the young man has to act in a certain way in the world in order to be accepted by his peers — that is, he must act confident, cool, experienced in love — when he may be feeling utterly terrorized inside. At this point in his development where he is struggling to make the transition from boyhood to manhood, exposure of inner feelings is extremely dangerous — after all, he is trying to show that now he really is a man.

Girls have a different experience. Because girls are allowed to have emotions and upsets and insecurities, adolescence is a time when they too need their friends. Girls spend much of their time in adolescence talking to and listening to each other in their pains and woes of love affairs, fights with parents, changing bodies. Girls use their relational skills to be with one another.

Because of this imbalance, once again girls continue to develop their nurturing potential whilst boys' emotions are locked inside themselves. Something important is learned about emotions through this experience. Because girls are surrounded by emotional chatter, dramas, sagas, they come to see that emotional upset passes. That is, it is something that is there, quite intensely, it is talked about, lived through with a friend, and then it is over. Learning to sit with someone else in their upset, listen and try to understand what it is they are going through (getting into their shoes so to speak) is another critical lesson in nurturance. Adolescent boys miss yet another chance to develop skills of equal emotional exchange, of giving and taking. The gap gets wider and men come to be frightened of emotions.

The imbalance in learning how to nurture means that a man comes to feel bewildered and confused about what it is he's supposed to do when demands are made of him to respond to his lover's emotional needs. Like Frank the lawyer, many men hear complaints by their partners that they are not giving in the right ways or that they don't listen adequately. Men are sensitive to such criticisms and more often than not respond with anger and frustration. 'What *do* women want?' 'I don't know what she wants from me. She's driving me crazy.' 'No matter what I do it's never the right thing. When Alice is upset she tells me I make her feel worse. I try to make suggestions about how she can get out of feeling depressed and she says I'm all wrong and that I don't understand anything. It's infuriating.' These kinds of statements are familiar to many heterosexual couples. Women feel men should understand and know what to do because the woman knows how to in the reverse situation. Women can't understand or believe that a man doesn't know what she wants; she feels he's just withholding and being impossible. The man, on the other hand, feels the woman is being impossible, insatiable and undermining. Nothing he can do is right. What happens at that moment?

Men expect to be listened to. It is in the very fabric of their experience that they can look to a woman to listen to them. Their mothers listened when they were boys, girlfriends listened when they were adolescents and women listen when they are men. Men look to women to validate themselves. They see themselves reflected in the adoring and awestruck eyes of the woman.[3] Men need this attention and confirmation of their worth. Very often men don't even want women to respond or give advice about something they are talking about — they just want to be listened to in the way their fathers were listened to. To be a man is to command attention and authority. Precisely because men have the continuity of being listened to, they believe that that is the way it should be.

It is tragic that, often, only through the loss of something do we become aware of having it to begin with. So for the little girl who has had the experience of being mothered and lost it, the taste of what was lingers on and women live in search of that contact, that care from their partner.

3. Often a woman only gets this kind of attention and appreciation of herself through being able to present herself as attractive and appealing.

Paradoxically, because men in a sense haven't lost 'it' they don't know 'it' exists. So when a man says to his lover, 'I don't know what it is you want that you're not getting,' he means it. He doesn't really know what he's supposed to be giving that he isn't giving. For the woman it often is terribly difficult to put into words what 'it' is that she feels he's not giving. She wants to be listened to, deeply, respectfully, seriously. She wants him to be attentive to her, to care about what she is going through emotionally, she wants care and concern and back-up in the world. She wants the 'woman' behind her in her life, supporting her success and development, and enabling her to be autonomous — the same 'woman' that a man has always had. Part of men's confusion about 'what *do* women want?' is symptomatic of their own experience and what they've been able to take for granted.

But what we have seen is that 'it' is not just there by nature or magic. It is there because our society raises girls to provide it. Mothers teach their daughters to provide nurturance just as their mothers before them, and mothers have been able to transmit something quite different to their sons. Because her son is not like her, because she knows he will not become a woman, a wife, a mother like her, a mother relates to her son with a range of conscious as well as unconscious ideas about what it means to be a man. Boys come to experience emotional nurturing as part of the fabric of life. It is one of those invisible 'laws' of patriarchal culture. Boys' and men's emotional dependency needs are less exposed and more continually met. Indeed, part of the reason that they are less exposed than women's is precisely because they are met on a more regular basis. Men more often than not do not have to crave emotional attention and connection because they receive it. They are given it by women who have been raised from their earliest days to supply it; to look to see what he's feeling, thinking, needing. Boys are not raised to develop the emotional antennae which girls acquire.

Men need women. Men more often than not search for a woman to care for them and love them. Men who are not in

relationships but who want to be are extremely lonely,
upset, in pain — just as women are in a similar situation. The
point we are attempting to uncover is the myth that men are
independent. That is one of the myths of patriarchy which
must be examined and challenged. Men and women alike
suffer from that myth. It makes everyone feel sick inside
because they know themselves to be dependent and yet this
very human emotion has been cast in such a bad light. In the
next chapter we will look at the interplay between men and
women in this most fundamental dynamic of dependency.

4

Dependency and Couples

The most powerful social model on which we base our lives is that of the heterosexual couple. The notion of a partner for life is introduced to us from early childhood when we become aware of our individual identity within society. It is then that we experience a split between our private and public worlds, and some of our internal experience becomes repressed. We unconsciously long to find a partner who will meet us in both worlds. As we grow up, we develop hopes, fantasies and expectations that one day we will have someone with whom we can share a special intimacy. Children's games reflect these hopes. We read about princes and princesses who at long last meet and live happily ever after. Even when a child grows up with parents who fight frequently and are unhappy in their marriage, expectations of a future happy coupling persist. Some parents may transmit to their children that they married the 'wrong' person, that they are unhappy because of the other person. This does not necessarily stop the child's later desire and search for a partner. The child may come to feel that if she or he finds the 'right' person it will all be different. They may find trust or intimacy difficult but the model of the couple will still be ruling their visions.

Yet marriage and the couple relationship are coming under enormous pressure in modern society. Threats such as nuclear war and the devastating rise in unemployment have created a climate in which emotions are taut, people are living constantly on a knife-edge. And much of this pressure devolves on to the family. In our everyday experience we build up frustration, but this is often not directed at the offending person or object, but is only released in the privacy of the family, where emotional back-up is available. Because our emotions, and the release of them, are so private, and because we experience so much emotional deprivation in many areas of our lives, there is an enormous amount of need brought to the couple relationship.

At the same time, the roles of men and women are changing because of the women's liberation movement; sexual politics and power relations in couples are being challenged. These broad social issues are having revolutionary effects on the institution of marriage, bringing to the fore many frustrations and dissatisfactions that were previously buried, or non-existent. Divorce rates have steadily risen, and fewer and fewer couples stay together for a lifetime. Yet the high divorce rate has not proved that people no longer believe in marriage. The rate of remarrying is also high. After the pain of separation, women and men continue the search for a new partner, a partner who will better meet their needs and make them feel fulfilled. The powerful image of the happy couple conquers disillusionment, and men and women continue to pursue the ideal of intimacy that has been instilled in them since childhood.

In the following pages, we examine particular couple relationships to see how dependency needs are revealed or concealed.

The Cha-Cha Phenomenon
It's Saturday afternoon. Janie and Peter are sitting in their living room reading. Janie looks over to Peter and feels waves of love for him. She loves the way he looks. She feels happy. She goes to sit next to him on the sofa, gives him a kiss. He looks up and smiles and looks back down at his book. Janie says, 'Maybe we should forget about going to the movies tonight and just make a nice dinner at home. We can open our good wine.' Peter responds, 'Well, I really do feel like seeing that movie.'

This is step one of the cha-cha. Janie feels open to Peter. She makes several gestures towards him for contact. The first 'rebuff' was Peter looking down at the book after the kiss. The second move away from intimate contact was his rejection of the 'dinner in' idea. Janie felt both of these gestures as rejection.

Step two of the cha-cha:

Janie gets up and moves back to her chair. She feels hurt. She has a twinge of anger. She gets back into reading her book. In the silence of their reading there is a slightly 'chilly' air between them. Janie does not look over and no longer feels filled with loving feelings as she did earlier.

Step three of the cha-cha:

Peter looks up from his book, yawns and stretches and looks over towards Janie. She doesn't look up despite the sounds made from his yawn. He says, 'Would you like a cup of coffee?'

Janie, still reading her book, says, 'No thanks.' Peter goes into the kitchen, makes the coffee. Calls to Janie from the kitchen, 'When do you think you'll want lunch, love?' Janie: 'Not yet.' Peter comes back out into the living room, goes over to Janie and gives her a kiss on the head. He sits himself on the arm of the chair and puts his arm around Janie. She looks up from her book, but not at Peter.

Peter becomes aware of the space between them which Janie's backing away in step two created. Feeling the space Peter moves towards Janie. There are now two possibilities for the next scene.

Possibility one: Janie, after a minute or two, looks at Peter, takes his hand, and 'comes back' to him. At this point the cha-cha is over. Perhaps Janie expresses some anger towards Peter and tells him that she felt hurt by his not wanting to stay in for the evening or pushed away when she approached him earlier on the couch. Or she may remain quiet and 'let go' of the hurt and anger and respond to Peter.

Possibility two: Janie continues to look at her book and through her silence and ignoring Peter lets him know that she is angry. He gets up from the arm of the chair and goes back to the couch and picks up his book, making a heavy sigh as he does this. They remain silent and the feeling in the room is

chilly and uncomfortable for both of them. The cha-cha
continues. At some point one of them will approach the
other and if there is a positive response the cha-cha will end.
If, on the other hand, the response is tentative or cold, it is
likely that the approaching partner will back off once again
only to wait for the other to make the next move. The cha-
cha continues.

This particular chain of events may occur in several
different forms. The basic form involves one partner
positively approaching the other in the pursuit of contact
and the other retreating. One person in the couple feels
loving, wants contact and closeness, makes moves towards
their partner and is met with a rebuff, a distancing gesture.
The reaction to this kind of rejection usually is a backing off,
a retreat by the partner who originally approached. This is
followed by a period of time (often quite brief) in which
both partners feel distant, followed by the original 'backing
away' partner moving towards the other in an effort to
retrieve him or her. The cha-cha phenomenon can occur
with one partner (partner A) regularly being the approaching one and partner B regularly being the retreating or
distancing one. It can occur with long intervals between the
shift from who is doing the approaching and who is doing
the backing-off (several days or weeks). It can occur in quite
an even balance between steps towards and steps away and
which partner is doing what step at what point.

Also varying within the cha-cha phenomenon is the length
of time the couple can sustain closeness and openness before
one thing or another creates distance between them. It can
take place in quite dramatic and explicit ways, and also
more subtly.

The cha-cha phenomenon is one way in which couples
display a fear of intimacy. It is as if being close and loving for
too long places one in jeopardy. One partner has to
disentangle and back away. The cha-cha comes as an
interruption into the intimacy. The reader may be thinking,
'Just because Peter didn't want to stay in that night, why
does that prove that he was retreating from intimacy? The

guy just wanted to see a film.' We'll tell you a bit more about Janie and Peter so that we can see that cha-cha within the context of their relationship and the dependency/intimacy issues they were struggling with.

Just around the time of the sofa incident, Janie and Peter had sought counselling. Peter felt that Janie was too dependent on him. He didn't like it that she needed him so much. He felt that she was too clingy and controlling. She organized their social plans and always seemed to him to be over-involved in the details and activities of his life. Janie, on the other hand, felt that Peter was often 'absent' emotionally, that he was unaware of and forgetful about these things. She felt that he didn't really take care of them himself so she had to pick up the pieces.

Because Peter felt taken over or controlled by Janie he distanced himself by creating boundaries in order to keep her out. Each time he distanced himself, Janie reacted to his distancing by trying to move closer. Each time she moved closer, Peter felt this to be her taking him over and he would move further away in an attempt to preserve himself. Each time he moved further and strengthened the boundaries between them, Janie felt this to be his being 'absent' and unaware of things around him in their lives together. Janie moving towards Peter in an attempt to get through his boundaries and Peter retreating further and further in an attempt to escape what he unconsciously felt to be Janie's intention to take him over or possess him was a central feature of their relating. The cha-cha phenomenon was just one of the outcomes. Only when Peter felt Janie to be distant from him, only when he felt the space and distance between them because she had backed away (emotionally), could he move towards her. Only when she was angry with him or hurt and withdrawn could he feel his feelings and need for her. He then could come towards Janie in the cha-cha. The cha-cha phenomenon works to keep an emotional distance between a couple. It adds an element of precariousness to a couple's life together; it makes both members somewhat on edge and dissatisfied and yet it is very prevalent. Could this be because it keeps us away from confronting directly the very complicated feelings that are hard to put into words concerning the fear of intimacy? If it is hard to face that confrontation, then the cha-cha, while distancing, has a function in keeping each member of the couple distanced enough to avoid that deeper fear.

Related to the cha-cha behaviour was Peter's repression of his own dependency needs when Janie was in pursuit of him. It was very difficult for him to negotiate feeling his need for Janie and then not feeling swamped by her in his vulner-ability. In the therapy it emerged that Peter loved and needed Janie very much. His distancing and aloof behaviour was a defence against his feelings of dependency. Janie's dependency and apparent clinging behaviour served an important function in the relationship. As long as Janie held on firmly to Peter and was 'overly' involved with him, he did not feel at all insecure. His own dependency needs were being met 'surreptiously' by Janie's appearing to need him so desperately. After all, if Janie was so dependent on Peter, she would never leave. He felt very secure.

This illustrates another central feature of dependency and its relation to intimacy. It is something we call *carrying the dependency*. Peter's desire to come to couple therapy was extremely positive because unconsciously he knew that he needed Janie to 'back off' or let go a bit, in order for him to be emotionally fulfilled in the relationship. He knew that he was emotionally going further and further away and couldn't help himself, even though he knew he didn't want to be. In the therapy we discovered reasons why Peter had come to feel that a woman could take him over or possess him and why he felt he had to create such firm boundaries between himself and his partner. Much of this had to do with his early upbringing and his relationship with his mother. In the therapy he was able to admit to his dependency needs and to feel that Janie wouldn't swallow him up because of this. Gradually, as Peter became less defensive, more able to show his love and more able to sustain close contact for longer periods of time, so too did Janie's clingy behaviour diminish. Because she no longer felt so pushed away by Peter and because she was able to feel more secure in his love for her, she was able to be more autonomous. She felt freer to make plans which didn't involve Peter and she had more trust that Peter was handling his own emotional affairs. She now felt that he was responsible and could maintain his own social contacts, so she no longer undermined him in these areas.

Within the couple relationship, the dissolving of barriers, the intimacy and the longing for closeness bring their own problems. Beginnings of relationships often seem so easy. There is usually terrific excitement, fluttery feelings, eagerness for sexual contact, lots of things to talk about with one another, desire to please the other by the way we dress, cook a meal, display attentiveness, etc. These beginnings of 'getting involved' seem almost effortless. For some couples, as time goes by, the sexual relationship and the channels of emotional understanding and communication get stronger and better. For many couples the love between two people grows and the connection deepens. For all couples there is some degree of friction and struggle. Disappointment and flare-ups happen as quickly as a flash of lightning, often for no apparent reason. Mood changes are affected dramatically and instantaneously. People unwittingly have impulses to control or direct their partner. Partners withdraw from one another emotionally and physically, only to return again to closeness. Some people feel that, as time passes, they have less to talk about with their partner than in the early years or that their sexual interest has diminished.

From all the nuances and complications of couple relationships one central question stands out: if people so obviously need and search for contact and emotional intimacy, why is it that achieving this intimacy is at times so difficult or, to be more to the point, why is it that once we achieve a certain level of intimacy it is so difficult to sustain?

The fear of intimacy is a very common but unrecognized phenomenon. Most people are not aware or conscious of it, but the vast majority of relationship difficulties have an element of this fear in them. The fear of intimacy is woven by many threads: the divorce between the public and private world; the psychological phenomenon of trans-ference; the narcissistic needs which drive us to seek to relate; the narcissistic gratifications we crave from one another. All these phenomena are created by our parenting and child-raising arrangements which bring particular pres-sures to our first love affair, the love we all experienced with our mothers, the blueprint for all our close relation-ships. Not only do we come from our mother's body where we were physically and therefore actually merged with her, but our psychological merger with our mother carried on into the first year of our lives. In previous chapters we have explained the way in which an infant, before developing a sense of self, is merged with its mother. That is, the infant feels her in its world; there are no boundaries and everything that comes into the infant's world feels in some sense as if it is a part of the infant itself. All of the early experiences of eating and taking in our mother's milk, feeling the warmth and comfort and satisfaction of that experience, are not erased from our memories. They are forgotten but they are not erased. Similarly all of the unpleasant and frightening and upsetting experiences — of hunger, pain, discomfort, yearning for contact and familiar smell, touch that is not there at the moment the infant is wanting it — are repressed or forgotten, but not erased from our psyches.

As adults there are certain experiences which generate feelings which we had in infancy. Some experiences resonate on a visceral level, or vaguely remind us of something we can't put our fingers on. What actually may be happening is that a deeply forgotten or buried memory is being touched, stirred.

Deep intimacy in adult relationships seems to touch many of the unconscious memories we have of our early intimate relationship with mother. In that relationship, let's not forget, she was extremely powerful in relation to us. We were dependent on her for our survival. She seemed to have a magical power with which she could either make the world safe and satisfying, or create an empty, frightening world where we feared for our very survival. As we developed we took in her caring and loving (as well as that of others) and we developed capabilities for becoming more autonomous. As toddlers grow and separate from mother, they become less dependent in certain kinds of ways. They begin to put spoons into their own mouths, they begin to walk enabling them to get about without being carried, etc. Each step is a step which takes us further from that original merger and utter dependency.

This is the stuff that the fear of dependency is made of. In our developing intimacy, both emotional and physical, with a lover, various psychological interactions take place which resonate at a deep level with that early experience of merger and dependency. People have an unconscious fear that through adult intimacy they will return to that early state where they were actually one with their 'partner' and in the merger they will be swallowed up and lost. Unconsciously they fear that they will not hold on to their sense of themselves as separate from their partner. A commitment and deep involvement with another stirs feelings of utter contentment, bliss and unity as well as feelings of being confined, restrained, imprisoned. For some people the negative aspects of the early merger that are recalled are so disturbing and unmanageable that they feel better in themselves when they are not in a relationship. They have a different experience of themselves, perhaps freer.

Let's take a closer look at some of the ways in which people protect themselves from this fear of intimacy.

Janet and Laurie met at a women-only bar. They became lovers and for several weeks spent almost twenty-four hours a day together. They enjoyed one another's company thoroughly and from the beginning felt a strong compatibility between them. Janet began to stay at Laurie's apartment four or five nights a week. On the mornings when Janet intended to go back to her own apartment after work Laurie

for one reason or another would be withdrawn, perhaps
irritated, generally in some kind of a bad mood. They would
leave each other feeling a bit distant. Even when they had
had an especially lovely and close time together on the
preceding days, inevitably they would part with less than
warm and loving feelings. This friction escalated to the point
where they would actually have arguments on the mornings
that Janet was going back to her flat. The pattern that
followed was that for that night they each, in their own
apartments, would feel terrible and somewhat angry with
the other; then the following day one would call the other,
they would make plans to get together either that night or
the next, and after being together for a couple of chilly hours
they eventually warmed up and had a loving and intimate
time together. This would follow for the two or three days
they stayed together and then the same pattern would repeat
itself all over again when Janet was leaving. When they
finally talked about it, what emerged was that Laurie
wanted them to live together and each time Janet went
home Laurie took this as a sign that Janet didn't want to be
with her as much as she wanted to be with Janet. Laurie felt
rejected and hurt and this was why she withdrew and acted
annoyed. She was trying to protect herself from Janet's
leaving by 'leaving' first.

In subtle ways Laurie carried the dependency feelings in
the relationship. Janet was able to come and go because
Laurie's dependency needs provided the base, the anchor
which helped Janet to feel very secure, loved and wanted
within the relationship. With those secure feelings she was
able to be away from Laurie and be involved in other
aspects of her life such as her work, her political meetings,
etc.

In Laurie and Janet's relationship there was both a
physical withdrawing — i.e. Janet going to her apartment —
and an emotional withdrawing — i.e. Laurie withdrawing
herself emotionally, becoming distant and irritated with
Janet on the mornings she left. The 'chilly' hours spent when
they got back together was the time when they both had to

renegotiate the emotional and the physical coming together again. It took a bit of time for Laurie to come out of herself again and to open up to Janet, to let her be close again emotionally. This couple thoroughly enjoyed their intimacy when they were together and open. The difficulties they experienced resulted from their partings. But, in another respect, Laurie always felt powerless in relation to Janet. She felt at Janet's mercy. Janet seemed to have control over the comings and goings and Laurie was emotionally on a see-saw, always being ready to prepare herself for the 'loss' of Janet. Janet seemed to be able to handle the brief separations without any difficulty. She seemed to stay intact throughout whilst Laurie felt emotional waves of invasion and loss. Psychologically Janet held the firm boundaries while Laurie held the needs.

It often appears that one partner in a couple is more dependent than the other. Usually these seem to be fixed positions, but there are times when they may shift back and forth. For the majority of couples it is the woman who appears to be the dependent one. Women are thought to be more 'clingy', needy and helpless. Women's emotional lives often seem to be much more caught up in their relationships than do men's. Men often appear more independent and secure within their relationships. In Chapter 3 we showed the ways in which men's dependency needs are often hidden from view because of their psychological development and their socialization to a male role. We showed the ways in which boys continue to receive maternal nurturance and do not have to give up their expectation of continued emotional nurturance and how this, in turn, makes them less emotionally hungry than women, less emotionally deprived. In Chapter 2 we showed that this experience is not parallel for a girl, who must give up her expectation of continued maternal nurturance in order to become a heterosexual woman in our society. We showed how girls come to feel deprived and hungry emotionally; how they come to feel that there is something wrong with them (in order to justify why they were pushed away by their mothers); how they come to feel as if their emotional needs are overwhelming and fear that perhaps there is an unending well of neediness inside which they must hide from others.

As we have said, because women come not to expect satisfactory emotional nurturance and understanding from their partners, men's inadequacy in giving this nurturance is to some extent accepted and even anticipated by women. In the beginning of a relationship, because of the heightened emotional activity which is a part of the 'courting' process, the partner appears to be caring. As time goes on and men's attentiveness wanes, women feel tremendous loss and disappointment. Women often express great disdain for men's ignorance in emotional matters. This contempt that women feel is rarely expressed directly. When women do express their needs it often comes out in the form of a criticism. A woman may suffer repeated disappointments because, although on one level she may accept that she won't get sufficient emotional attention and care, on another level she fights this knowledge because she still feels such great need. The woman may declare that she doesn't feel happy in the relationship, that she feels her partner doesn't give enough emotionally and so on. He wants her to be more specific, he doesn't know what she's talking about. He responds to the criticism with anger, which to some degree frightens her. She finds it hard to be more specific; why doesn't he know what she means; how come he doesn't understand this; she understands and intuits what he feels even when he doesn't put it perfectly into words; and so on. She also begins to feel shaky because her most feared fantasy is actually happening. She is being pushed away and rejected because her needs are exposed. She hears him say that she's too needy, that he doesn't know what she wants, that no matter what he does it's never right, and she feels this to be true too. The fight is often resolved in the following way. She cries and backs off, taking the bad feelings into herself, feeling that once again her anger was impotent, feeling defeated and in despair that she will never get what she needs and that it's just as much her fault as his because she doesn't even know what it is she wants. He gives her a hug and a kiss and as he does this she feels better. They make up. Until next time. He feels relieved that it's over and that it was to do with all of her over-neediness and really not much to do with his behaviour. He may have a slight twinge of guilt, although it feels diffuse and he can't really pinpoint what it's about. He may feel unhappy that she was so upset.

But the psychological catch is that the woman feels that her needs are too great, and so the defences that the man has constructed against his own feelings of inadequacy in the arena of emotional nurturance, and his defences against feeling his 'femininity', seem necessary because of what appears to be the woman's insatiability. It is not seen as his not knowing how to give adequately, but that she wants too much. The woman's psychology prepares her to collude in this fiction and to protect her man from these feelings of inadequacy. She does not want to expose his 'weakness' and vulnerability because then she loses the illusion of this being the person who can love and take care of her. She looked for someone to 'replace' her mother, she hoped she had finally found a person who would love and care for her again, and therefore she joins with him in hiding from view the fact that he may not be able to provide this nurturance. If she exposes that he can't, then she feels bereft and alone once again.

The man who is unconsciously trying to repress his 'femininity' and his early involvement with his mother cannot psychologically afford to have his woman trying to expose that part of him. *Psychologically the man is in a terrible bind. On the one hand he must repress this aspect of his personality* (which has been stifled from early development) *in order to be a man, and at the same time in a loving relationship he must draw on this part of himself*. In order for a man to give the very things a woman feels are lacking, the contact that a woman wants, he is involved in a process that directly threatens his conception of self.

Ilene and Thomas were married for twenty-three years. When they first met they thought the world of each other.

Ilene, who had not had a very loving family background, felt at long last that she had someone who would really love her. Thomas was handsome and charming, he had a growing business and he treated Ilene gallantly. She was utterly devoted to him. Over the years of their marriage Ilene catered to Thomas's desires, trying to be a super-wife. She decorated the house elegantly, prepared gourmet dishes for dinner, worked at keeping her body trim and pleasing to Thomas and was hostess to his business affairs. They had two children. When Thomas went away on business trips Ilene wanted him to call her each day. She felt she needed that contact and wanted to know that he was all right. When she would ask him questions about these small trips he would get irritated. He wanted to know why she wanted to know these things, why she was always having to involve herself in all aspects of his life. Ilene felt rejected and upset; she began to feel that Thomas was hiding something from her. She began to feel suspicious about where he was whenever he was away from her. She asked his secretary lots of questions about his luncheon dates and business meetings. She felt herself becoming more and more insecure, nervous and clingy. She couldn't imagine what she would ever do without Thomas; he was her life; she lived for him. She continually vowed to herself not to ask Thomas questions about who was at the meeting, where it was being held, etc. Each time she did he became furious with her and yet each time it seemed to slip out of her before she could catch herself. During an argument which followed one of these exchanges Thomas told Ilene 'not to push him'. She felt frightened. What did he mean by that? Was he planning on leaving her? She had better be careful and keep her upset to herself and act like everything was fine, loosen the reins, not ask questions. One evening Ilene's friend Roseann saw Thomas at a restaurant with a woman. She told Ilene about it. Ilene's world collapsed. This is what she had known deep down inside her for some months, this is what she had been trying to find out from Thomas and now she finally knew. When he came home that evening she confronted him with the information. He said that it was true and that he wanted to stay with Ilene but he wouldn't stop seeing the other woman; they had become too involved. Ilene said that she couldn't live like that and after much pain and anger, they decided to separate. For the next six months Ilene suffered terribly. She felt herself lost at the bottom of the sea. Her children, now twenty and sixteen, felt sorry for her and angry with their father. Then Ilene woke up one day and decided that she could not remain in the house they had shared for so many years. She wanted to live and get her own apartment. She was starting to feel better; she had to go on with her life and she had to move herself out of Thomas's surroundings. She found a lovely apartment and moved in. She decorated it just the way she liked and actually had moments of exuberance and joy about what she was creating. Meanwhile, the children saw their father irregularly, but each time they saw him they reported on how Ilene was doing. In the period when Ilene was feeling stronger and developing her own life apart from Thomas, Thomas decided to visit her. He had only seen her once months earlier when she was extremely depressed. Ilene felt shocked to see Thomas. She felt quite shaken but tried very hard not to show this to him. She showed him the apartment and talked about the various things she had done in fixing it up. She told him how she was beginning to look for work. Thomas felt himself attracted to Ilene. When he left he felt shaken and upset. Over the next few days he thought about Ilene often. He wanted to see her again. It wasn't until Ilene appeared not to need him so desperately that he became aware of the fact that he hadn't let go of her at all in his own mind, that over the period of the separation, somewhere in the back of his mind he still felt Ilene was there. He felt that she needed him so badly that he could always go back to her. As she began really to separate from him emotionally and turn her energies towards herself and outward elsewhere, he became frightened and aware of his own dependency on Ilene.

In all the years of their marriage Ilene had appeared to be

the dependent partner. She held firmly to Thomas and because she held firmly he felt secure. This fitted with his upbringing which informed him that as a man he should not be dependent, that dependency meant weakness, and meant in effect that Thomas did not feel his own dependency needs. All of the ways in which he depended on Ilene for his daily care, for her listening and concern, for her support of his success, for her raising his children, for her providing him with sexual pleasure and satisfaction, for her caring for his home, his clothes, were hidden and taken for granted. To everyone including Ilene and Thomas it looked like she was the dependent partner. It wasn't until Ilene began to feel really separate from Thomas, eight months after the physical separation, that he was forced to feel his dependency. Up until that point, even in their physical separation, he still needed to feel that Ilene was emotionally there for him.

Thomas exemplifies the advantages men experience in a patriarchal society as well as the disadvantages. He was respected and looked after in ways that gave him the status of king in his own home. He was a successful man. His emotional and physical dependency needs continued to be met. Being raised as a man, Thomas unconsciously came to expect such treatment and so had little difficulty in accepting this luxurious attention. He felt he deserved it and he took it all in without difficulty. But Thomas's problem was his inability to show or accept his emotional vulnerability. Showing love or dependency seemed to him a great weakness. His emotions felt infantile to him, and he could not tolerate them. He needed Ilene to carry all of the dependency in the relationship because he could not afford to exhibit any of his own. Emotions felt feminine and Thomas was a man. Dependency and intimacy are closely related. Closeness and contact with another may make one feel vulnerable. Many people have difficulty in showing their love or affection because they feel too vulnerable and worry that they may be rejected or thought to be silly by the other. People often keep their feelings of love inside in an attempt to protect themselves from anticipated hurt and rejection. We have the ability to create invisible boundaries between us and others to hide this fear. Sometimes we can control when these boundaries are up and when we can let them down and allow for closeness. Often these boundaries feel like they have a will of their own and even though we may want to say, 'I love you,' or we may want to take our lover's hand in ours, we feel paralysed. The boundaries not only keep the other person out but they also hold us back. We can sometimes feel imprisoned by our boundaries, which keep us from achieving the intimacy we long for.

Showing love, exposing our need and desire for contact, touches our feelings of dependency. Letting ourselves feel our wants for another person is a kind of letting go. It is a giving of ourselves. Emotional dependency, needing, wanting and giving love to another person is the fabric of intimate relationships. In their emotional lives people are both strong and sensitive. Loving someone and feeling emotionally vulnerable to them is both effortless and painstaking. It is the easiest thing in the world and the most difficult. We long for intimacy and we fear intimacy.

When we are involved in a relationship our emotional channel is on fine tuning. We feel disappointment at the smallest thing. We are so tuned in to our partner psychologically, that their behaviour or even their mood affects the way we ourselves feel. Let's take a step back to the beginning of a relationship to find what makes for the fine-tuning in intimate relationships.

Falling in Love

What attracts two people to each other? Why do certain physical types attract certain people and other physical types others? Are there matches 'made in heaven'? Upon first meeting one sees only a handful of things about another person. We see the way a person is dressed, what their face looks like, their physical presence. Many people find themselves drawn to a particular physical type, be it tall, short, thin, stocky, long-haired, fair-haired, dark. etc.

When people meet there is usually some aspect of the other that attracts them to that person. If the attraction is mutual there is a spark and contact is made. At the very beginning of a relationship two people actually know very little about one another. The process of getting to know someone is an intricate one. In a relatively short time one can learn about someone else's background, their family, their class, education, where they grew up, what their occupation is and so on. It takes quite a lot longer, however, to begin to be *intimate* with another person.

Although it takes time to develop intimacy, it is the exception rather than the rule today that two people who are attracted to each other first take time to get to know the other and then 'fall in love'. Most often, people seem to 'fall in love' early on in the relationship and get to know each other later. Indeed, it might be said that falling in love is the first step required in pursuing a relationship. Of course, there are couples who have known each other a number of years,[1] perhaps they have been friends, and eventually they become lovers, so that the falling in love happens after the knowing, but this is unusual.

Hollywood has filled our minds and hearts with images of love at first sight. Two people spot each other across a crowded room and their eyes meet. Music streams from the heavens, filling us with the magic of the moment. Countless couples over the decades have found each other on the screen and at that powerful moment we all feel that this is what we, too, have been waiting for — the moment is deep inside us. Fred Astaire and Ginger Rogers have at last found the partner they have been waiting for — the answer to their dreams and the resolution to their lives. They glide across the floor together perfectly in step and filled with the joy that this is the best that life offers.

At the risk of blowing apart the mystique that surrounds falling in love or bursting the bubble of romance we'd like to take a closer look at this phenomenon of falling in love.

1.   Historical changes are discussed in Chapter 5.

There are many levels to this attraction, some which have to
do with the qualities we actually see in the other person and
some which have more to do with our own psychology and
who we need the other person to be. Various psychological
dynamics such as transference, projection, narcissistic identification, mirroring may at any point be a part of the
relating process.

Narcissistic Needs

Alison meets Jack at a party. She is attracted to him. She
thinks that he is a great dancer and very good-looking. He
has dark eyes which she notices immediately. He smiles at
her and they begin to talk. Jack is comfortable and friendly.
He seems very at ease with himself and appears to be a
gentle person. Alison feels herself falling in love. In bed that
night Alison can't stop thinking about Jack. She imagines
him meeting her friends and family and being very charming
and everyone loving him. She feels she could be with him
forever.

Alison doesn't know Jack. They spent all of twenty
minutes talking to one another at the party. How do we
explain the fantasies that Alison had about her life together
with Jack? Fantasy plays a big part in falling in love because
at the very beginning we have all of our needs and we are
psychologically 'ready' to have a person come along to fit in
with and meet them. Fantasies are within our control. We
create them to soothe ourselves, stimulate ourselves, upset
ourselves; we can create good endings and bad endings; we
can create joyful moments and deeply distressing ones.
Although she had friends and family who cared about her,
Alison had an unsettled feeling deep inside. Jack was warm
and friendly and gentle. Alison's brief interaction with Jack
and her experience of these qualities in his personality
touched her yearning and her hope that here was a person
who could meet her needs. In the forefront of Alison's
fantasies were her needs and longings and in the background
were the particulars of who Jack actually was. On an unconscious level Alison felt she needed someone to fill the

emptiness she felt inside. Somewhere along the line in Alison's early psychological development she did not secure and internalize a firm sense of self. She wanted him because of her own emptiness. She was relating out of a narcissistic need.

Another example of a narcissistic need is one person wanting contact with another because of a characteristic they possess which the person feels to be missing in her or himself. So, for example, Daniel, an extremely introverted and shy man, fell in love with Cynthia, who on the surface was extremely friendly, warm and giving. She was always able to make people feel at ease and social situations were comfortable and easy for her. Through Daniel's relationship with Cynthia he was able to feel that he now possessed some of those qualities which he had lacked. Some of Cynthia's outgoingness seemed to rub off on him. He felt more secure in social situations when she was with him. In this relationship the narcissistic need actually worked both ways because Cynthia, in fact, was quite out of control and 'all over the place'. She did not feel a clear sense of her own boundaries. She found it impossible to say 'no', for example, and was so involved in other people's needs and wants that she was not 'living in her own skin'. In her relationship with Daniel (a person with rigid boundaries) Cynthia unconsciously utilized his boundaries for her own sense of containment.

Like Cynthia and Daniel, couples often seem to 'fit'. What these two saw as complementary personalities were in fact more than that. They each responded out of unconscious needs to the attributes and psychological make-up of the other. The power of the unconscious in our search for and choice of partner is sometimes astonishing. The expression 'a match made in heaven' describes a fit that works well. Two people come together each with their own psychology, their own emotional history and development, their own needs and expectations and ability to be in a relationship.

Narcissistic Identification

We all have aspects of our personalities which we like and those which we don't like. Sometimes we try to hide as best we can those aspects which we think are unpleasant or ugly. One way of ensuring that these aspects stay out of sight is to be involved with people who seem to have the attributes with which we prefer to identify. That is, we may like to be with people who seem to be the way we would like to be. We may like someone because of the way they dress, the way they look, the kind of work they do, the way they think about things, their political perspectives, the kind of car they drive, their taste in food, their cultural interests, sports interests, etc. We wish to get closer to that person because we like all kinds of things about them. Often these things either mirror aspects of ourselves which we like or they may represent the way we strive to be. Narcissistic identifications in couples may emerge after a time in a relationship and become apparent in the form of suddenly feeling upset or critical about a partner's character. Often it appears in quite trivial ways. For example, six months into their relationship Rena found herself disturbed by Al's bell-bottom trousers which she thought to be too wide and out of fashion. Every time she saw him wearing the wide bell-bottoms she found herself turned off and somewhat distant and irritated by him all evening. Rena's unconscious narcissistic identification with Al was such that she could not tolerate his appearing in a way which did not accurately reflect the way *she* wanted to look and wanted to be seen. Many people feel extremely sensitive to how others see and think about their partner. One may be concerned with the way their partner talks about various topics in a social situation — are they saying it right, are they saying the right things, does everyone think this person is witty, weird, etc. We begin to see our partner as an extension of ourself. When we imagine other people to be judging our partner, it feels as if *we* are being judged.

In relationships people become psychologically merged. This merger can happen in 'healthy' ways. Many aspects of couples' daily life represent merger. Setting up a home

together, buying furniture to share and creating a shared
living space is one example; sharing money is another —
money representing merger or separateness is very common; the way couples deal with money can say an awful lot
about how their relationship works — cooking and eating
food together, sharing cupboards, towels and so on. In many
ways sharing is an extremely pleasurable experience. It
represents a letting-go of a firmly fixed position of 'mine'. If
one feels secure enough in oneself, then sharing does not
seem threatening. Through a secure sense of selfhood one
can move into the world of 'mature' relationships and
tolerate more easily differences in one's partner — even
differences that one doesn't like. If one's partner likes to eat
red licorice in a roomful of one's friends who are gourmet
cooks this can be tolerated, without feeling the need to hide
the licorice, or pray that they don't eat it there for fear that
somehow the friends will think badly of one's partner and
therefore badly of oneself. Discomfort in the 'merger' stems
from the feeling that our partner is an extension of ourselves.
We try to control ourselves in all kinds of ways in order to
appear 'acceptable'. We then find ourselves trying to control
our partners in order to have them also appear 'acceptable'.
In these times when the world may seem less and less of a
safe place, we are thrown back on ourselves. Our in-
dividuality and our personal lives seem to be the only things
we can even hope to have some control over. Through
distorted lenses we meticulously observe ourselves to see
that everything is in order. This phenomenon extends to the
couple relationship, where our lovers as narcissistic ex-
tensions of ourselves are also under the critical magnifying
lens.

Transference
A person's emotional make-up, their psychology, of course
greatly influences their choice of partner. People bring a
whole range of unconscious expectations that were experienced in earlier relationships to adult relationships. This
is what Freud called 'transference'. He discovered in the

analytic relationship that his patients were unconsciously acting towards him as if he were their father or mother. They expected him to act and react in specific ways, reproducing the ways in which a parent acted. This happens to a great extent in all kinds of relationships. It is often a revelation to a man married for several years suddenly to realize that his wife is just like his mother in central ways. It is even more shocking when a woman realizes that her husband is just like *her* mother in many ways! In the early phase of a relationship the transference either 'works' or it doesn't. Someone may have a negative transference for instance, where they experience a partner's behaviour reflecting the most dreaded characteristics of a parent, cutting the possibility of the continuation of that relationship. For example, Janis met Robert at a bar. They chatted for a while and Robert asked to go out with Janis again. The next time they went out Janis decided that she really didn't like him. She couldn't quite pinpoint why this was so because the evening had superficially seemed quite nice. When Janis talked about this during her therapy and wondered why it was that she didn't like him she found herself describing his joke-telling. She remarked that he had told many brief jokes over the evening and that, although at the time she laughed, something about it bothered her. She then remembered the way in which her father had tried to get people to laugh a lot of the time and how she often felt embarrassed by his behaviour. She felt upset knowing that her father was needing the attention and was trying so desperately to be liked. She found it sad and it filled her with feelings of pity for him. She realized that the reason she didn't 'go' for Robert was that she superimposed this same quality on to him just because of the joke-telling. This is transference. In fact Janis didn't know Robert well enough and therefore had no idea what his joke-telling was about, but in his behaving in a way that reminded her of her father she (unconsciously) superimposed a whole set of other emotional characteristics on to him that actually belonged to her father's personality. Transference can destroy a potential relationship, but it also operates to cement relationships in both healthy and unhealthy ways.

Rosemary and Neil have been together for ten years. Neither of them feels really good about the relationship. Although they manage to have some good times, for the most part they feel dissatisfied. And yet they stay together. Neil is very withholding and for almost all of the ten years has tried to maintain a certain position of privacy within the relationship. He responds to Rosemary's questions with irritation and annoyance as if everything she asks is a demand. Emotionally and sexually he is very rejecting. In Rosemary's therapy she became aware of how by living with Neil she keeps reliving over and over again the rejections she felt from her mother. Rosemary lived with a continual feeling of deprivation and emotional hunger. She always felt as if things were her fault and that she wanted too much. She also felt as if there was something wrong with her, that she was undesirable, or else why didn't these people (Neil and her mother) love her more and give her more attention and care? Being related to in this way was so familiar to Rosemary that the prospect of things being different was actually quite scary. Holding on to the 'bad' attention at some level felt safer than letting go of it. She didn't know what else could replace it. Being involved with her 'mother' despite all the pain, hurt and anger that that brought with it felt less frightening psychologically than breaking free of the connection. Rosemary's putting up with Neil's continual rejection was satisfying an unhealthy seed. She was also still living with her 'mother'.

Transference in relationships can cross sex. In Rosemary's case there was a mother transference in operation. The equation can include any number of possibilities — mother-daughter, father-daughter, mother-son, father-son. Sometimes one is drawn to an aspect of another that reminds one of a sister, a brother, an aunt or uncle, a nanny or early childcare person other than mother. Transference can take many forms, and may be based on attraction because of physical or psychological traits. A person's new partners may, indeed, have similar qualities so the reader might ask 'Isn't it those real traits that the person is reacting to?' But the significance of the transference is all of the meaning and the range of feelings that one attributes to those particular traits. There can be a wealth of associations and expectations attached to a particular trait. For instance, Rebecca loves it that Larry sings to her. When she was a little girl her mother used to sing to her and so she finds Larry's singing comforting. It is not just Larry singing in the present that fills Rebecca with warm and cosy feelings. It is the powerful resonance at a subconscious level that produces those feelings in her. The fact that Rebecca then unconsciously relates to Larry in many other ways as if he were her mother is all a part of the transference operating in their relationship.

Coming to terms with the fact that one's partner is *not* one's mother or father and therefore does *not* respond as did they creates the possibility of individuals changing and growing emotionally. One may feel pleasantly surprised by a response one's partner has had to something one has done. The surprised feeling is the signpost to the transference — the unconscious expectation that there would be a different response. For example, when Rosa first started living with Bruce she noticed that, if she missed the 5.30 p.m. train home from work and reached the house twenty minutes later because she caught the 6.00 p.m. train, she would feel anxious from 5.20 p.m. until she saw Bruce. At those times he would get home just before her, at 6.15 p.m. Each time Bruce greeted her lovingly she felt relieved and thankful, but she didn't know why this was. In thinking about this, Rosa realized that as a girl whenever she came home from school even a few minutes later than expected, or when she visited a friend after school and got home slightly late for dinner, her mother would be furious with her. She would be met at the door with anger and her mother would treat her quite coldly for several hours thereafter. Each time Bruce greeted her lovingly she was somewhat shocked because unconsciously, and because of the transference in the close relationship, Rosa expected Bruce to react just as her mother had. After several months of their living together, Rosa's anxiety at missing the 5.30 p.m. train began to diminish. This particular development affected other aspects of their relationship and of Rosa's psychology. There were many ways in which Bruce's less rigid (less rigid than Rosa's mother's) expectations and controls and fears within the relationship helped Rosa to relax and to be less hard on herself, less punishing.

Sometimes a person may unconsciously try to provoke her or his partner into responding just like a father or mother did in the past. Getting a different reaction doesn't satisfy a deeply held conception. If one needs to 'do battle' with a parent because as an adult one still feels left with all sorts of psychological 'unfinished business', then a way to make this happen is to do the battle with the new partner. So, for example, George saw a pattern to his fights with Marion. Each time Marion criticized him for being too selfish and unaware of ways in which he ignored or hurt her they would have a big argument. George said that he at first felt defensive because he was being accused of being 'bad', but at the same time or just moments thereafter he felt guilty because he knew she was right. The yelling and screaming that followed in their fights ended up with Marion telling George what an awful person he was. Marion meanwhile felt extremely upset about how ugly their fights got at these times. George began to sense that somehow he provoked Marion until he escalated the fight to that painful level. Marion's original criticism might have been terribly small and insignificant but George took it and blew it up into something that he knew had little to do with Marion. It had to do with himself. He wondered why he seemed to steer their fights in the same direction time and time again. In analysing the transferential aspects of their relationship it became clear that George was fighting a continuing battle that he had had with his father with Marion. George's father often made him feel, as a boy, that he had disappointed him. George would feel terribly ashamed and guilty. He developed a poor self-image. Deep inside he felt he was not good enough. He saw himself through his father's eyes and always fell short of what was expected of him. In his relationship with Marion, George unconsciously continued the battle with his father. Each time Marion said that she didn't like the way he had behaved, that triggered a well of feelings inside him. He brought their fights to terribly painful levels where he would feel as if he was receiving a beating from Marion. He would be getting Marion to beat him psychologically because he was not good enough.

Transference, narcissistic identification or narcissistic need are not all there is to falling in love. At the beginning of an intimate relationship there are two people, each with their own unique psychology and history, who come together to enjoy, share, exchange with, care for, relate to and experience each other. When another person who one is attracted to responds favourably (for whatever reasons) and reciprocates loving feelings, it can be a transforming experience. Receiving love and feeling and giving love, whether it comes from conscious or unconscious resources, is a deep human need and activity. In most relationships there is at least a thread of newness, a reaching outward in an attempt to become involved with another person. Every relationship has aspects which can be seen as 'neurotic', but relationships are multi-dimensional. Even in what may appear to be the most 'unhealthy and neurotic' of relationships when one scratches beneath the surface the need and desire for human contact is always there.

Dependency in relationships also is multi-dimensional. In many ways just being in a couple satisfies dependency needs regardless of how much care and emotional involvement the two people may have. There are couples who to a large extent meet one another's dependency needs in direct and equal ways. There are couples who remain married for a lifetime and truly share their lives with one another, all the struggles as well as the joys. But there are many couples for whom the very existence of the relationship is paramount. We saw in Rosemary's case that, while she actually received little nurturing from Neil, on another level her dependency needs were being met to some extent within the relationship. But her lack of psychological and emotional separation from her mother meant that some of her dependency needs were still unfulfilled. The needs were met in form, by being married, but not in content. If the reader can remember Chapter 2, in Margaret and Robert's relationship there was a similar phenomenon. For many years Margaret and Robert stayed together despite the daily dissatisfactions they each felt. Experiences and relationships that each of them had in their infancy and childhood shaped their adult psychologies and those psychologies influenced them to stay in that relationship for a lifetime. There was, so to speak, a fit.

Loving relationships are a complicated mixture of dependency, intimacy, psychological yearnings and fears. In the next chapter we take a look at how these themes are expressed in the sexual aspects of intimate relationships.

5

Sex and Dependency

Our attitudes about sex and sexuality make for a complex and contradictory tapestry. So much of what we feel and think about sex is informed by prejudice of one kind or another. Often we aren't sure what we really believe. The subject touches raw nerves running along emotional tributaries. Sometimes we are open and receptive, at other times inexplicably defensive. Daily we are bombarded by different images of sexuality. Sex is used to sell toothpaste; to cement marriage; to stem anxiety; to make babies; to provide reassurance; to show love; to exercise power. Many unlikely objects are linked with sex. If the object is inanimate, such as a car, the sexual association humanizes it, imbues it with sexual vitality. At the same time, sex itself becomes stripped of its humanity and appears as a commodity, a thing to be had.

It is easier to describe sex and sexuality as it appears in particular examples than to pick it up and say, this is what it is. The difficulty is compounded by the fact that our notion of sexuality is a changing one. In recent history we have become a prurient society. The attitudes we have acquired are faintly dirty and quasi-religious. We are curious and hesitant.

Our parents' generation grew up with a more uniform view of sex than we have. There were good women and there were loose women. Men were required to be 'experienced' for their virgin brides. Homosexuality was hidden and denied, childhood was innocent. Pre-marital sexual conduct was regulated in dating rituals. Extra-marital sex was furtive. There were rules about what to do, how far to go, who to tell, and the ever-present threat of unwanted pregnancy — the supreme announcement of rebellion, disgrace, wantonness. The female was always perceived as the loser, the one to be pitied. Sex was trouble, female sexuality dangerous. If you were smart, you necked. You kept your desires in tow. You held on to the prize you could give your husband — your 'unsullied' body. You married, felt disappointed if the sexual relationship did not offer all it had promised. You wondered why you waited. Felt cheated and frustrated. You made a bargain — you accepted marriage, protection, a home. You taught your daughter to do as you did. And then Kinsey[1] wrote about you and your sexual experiences. He spoke frankly about your real experiences. And you wanted more and asked for it and then Masters and Johnson[2] responded. Your son and daughter had access to the pill. They talked free love and sometimes practised it. Sex was out of the closet. Professionals extolled the virtue of it. Older people went for sex counselling, young people experimented, palaces of sexual pleasure opened, sexual swinging became a pastime, women started sleeping with each other openly, and homosexual men moved to New York and San Francisco to create communities.

The result is that sex and sexuality are paradoxically *more* confusing today. We are encouraged to have an active sexual life and we believe it is a good idea. We are exhorted to enjoy sex, physical contact, massage, pleasure, to feel comfortable within our bodies and to have liberal views about our children's sexuality. And yet these possibilities, which we may endorse, bring with them a kind of pressure. As they and our inner thoughts and desires come together, we may feel bewildered and unclear about what we want and what it all means. We may feel that we put 'too much stress on sex' or

1.   A. Kinsey et al., *Sexual Behaviour in the Human Male*, Philadelphia 1948. A. Kinsey et al., *Sexual Behaviour in the Human Female*, Philadelphia 1953.
2.   W. Masters & V. Johnson, *Human Sexual Response*, Boston 1966.

'not enough'. We don't know if it is about love, eroticism, passion, involvement, tenderness, self-expression, reproduction, dependency, strength, power, and so on. It may be all of those things at different times. Sex has the power to please us more profoundly than we can put into words, or to alienate and disappoint. Our range of responses depends on our emotional state, and that of our partner(s), our physical well-being and our personal histories. Each of us has a sexual heritage which is unique. But obviously how we feel and think about our bodies and our sexuality reflects our gender and the sex roles we have absorbed.

Eleanor was a virgin until she married Jim in 1959. This was important to both of them as was the fact that he was 'experienced'. They didn't question this imbalance, it was just the way things were. Eleanor was 'keeping herself' for Jim. Jim wanted his wife to be 'pure'. Let's examine for a moment this notion that has left its mark on all of us. What do these two sentences tell us about sexuality in a heterosexual couple? The sexual relationship is cast in terms of ownership and possession. Eleanor delivered her sexuality to her husband. Jim, by marrying her, made her sexuality legitimate. For if she had acted on her sexual desires outside marriage, or if she had not been a virgin, she would have been regarded as somewhat 'tainted' and 'dirty' and *she herself would have felt this*. It is still true to some extent, as it was then, that when a man marries, he takes responsibility for his wife's sexuality. In a curious way, it now attaches to him, rather than to her. He has rights to it and the responsibility of being experienced. The father must give his daughter away to his son-in-law intact. Her sexuality passes from one man's protection to another's. In exchange for bringing her husband her sexuality, Eleanor expected to be economically supported. She in turn would take on the household tasks and the emotional realm of their life together.

Jim had been raised to anticipate regular sex as one of the benefits that went along with being grown up and married.

His sexual adventures up to his marriage had a particular
purpose. He wanted experience, although what that entailed
or meant was never quite spelled out. Eleanor grew up
intrigued by her sexuality, this quasi-dangerous magical
'thing' she had to watch out for. She thought of sexuality in
terms of love and commitment. Jim thought of sexuality in
terms of sensation and a good time. Eleanor and Jim are
typical of white middle-class people born in the late 1930s
and '40s who came of age before the 'sexual revolution' of
the late '60s. Their sexual life gradually became less satisfying to them after the first five years of their marriage.
They continued to be physically attracted to each other but,
after the children were born, their sexual contact settled into
a routine in which they were sexually intimate about twice a
month — a frequency judged to be inadequate by both of
them. They were physically aware of each other in a cosy
taken-for-granted way but both felt that was more affec-
tionate than sexual. Their teenage children's explorations
put them both through an emotional wringer, because they
didn't want to stand in the way of the children's adventures.
They both believed that their sexuality was somewhat
limited by how they had been brought up. They had spent
the first years of marriage trying to unravel the restrictions,
taboos and the ordinary ignorance they had both accrued.
They saw themselves as broadminded and liberal and they
were hesitant about interfering in their children's affairs, but
they were troubled by the kinds of sexual scenes they
imagined or knew that their kids were involved in. They
came for counselling to sort out how best not to interfere
with the kids and improve their own sexual life.

What they said about their sexual histories has been told to
us in its general points many times before. When Eleanor
and Jim made love for the first time, and by this they meant
intercourse, they already knew each other very well. They
had been dating for three years, were entwined in each
other's lives and had made decisions together about the
future. Jim was training to be an electrical engineer and
Eleanor decided to become a nutritionist because it would

offer flexibility and the possibility of part-time work for when she would start a family. Their own families got to know each other quite well and for a time Jim's cousin dated Eleanor's younger sister. When Jim and Eleanor married and set up house together they were deeply in love and couldn't wait to show this fully. Although they were both nervous about their first night together, they approached it with tremendous joy, free of guilt or anxiety. Like the vast majority of people, their sexual relationship was only one current within a much larger relationship that had developed between them. Expressing sexual love with each other without interruption was a logical climax to the emotional terrain they had tilled and nurtured over three years. Their sexual love brought them even closer. They felt deeply involved with and committed to each other. During love-making they were so utterly engrossed with each other that they remembered not knowing whose body was whose; and the intimacy that crossed physical boundaries created new psychological states in both of them and between them. They felt physically fused and totally absorbed by the sensuality they were creating together. Their sexual relationship became a means of communication for them. They stopped being so concerned with the more routine aspects of daily life — they didn't fill each other in on the details of what was happening at work and so on — their energy was drawn to romantic dinners followed by enraptured love-making and conversations in bed in which they couldn't take their eyes or hands off each other. They wondered why anyone did anything else but make love all day. Their sexual relationship brought a new and deeper state of intimacy, and they became dependent on their sexual relationship to express how they felt about each other. The sex took on particular emotional resonances and, tied together in this new way, they exposed their vulnerabilities and the parts of them hidden from the world. They had created a safe, exciting and mutually satisfying haven.

The exploits of their children shocked them. They found the contrast between the meaning that they had attached to

sex and sexuality and the seemingly cavalier attitude their
kids affected difficult to reconcile. This discordance within
the family led them to reflect on how they saw and
experienced their own sexual relationship after eighteen
years of married life. They began to face the fact that over
the last several years they had become somewhat dissatisfied and disappointed with their sexual life. It didn't feel as
expressive, as romantic, as exciting, as meaningful, as
crucial. The sex itself had become unimaginative. The time
before and after sex was not particularly special, the sex
neither followed especially good contact, nor opened up the
way for it. There was, they both agreed, a comfortable,
familiar feel about it. Their sexual communication did not
seem to reach them as deeply as in the past. It was reassuring
and reasonably enjoyable but did not stand for or signify a
particularly meaningful loving exchange.

We shall examine later on the developments that often
occur in relationships that bring the people involved to a
similar point that Eleanor and Jim reached. But for now
let's look in more detail at how the psychological themes
described in the previous chapter can deepen our understanding of the dynamics within this kind of sexual situation.

When a man and a woman make love in the context of an
intimate relationship, they are bonding together and creating something new and bigger than each of them. Their
sexual intimacy is more than an appetite, it is a creative act in
which each one is giving and being responsive. The desire to
make love arises out of the need to express love physically.
The physical and emotional boundaries between two people
temporarily dissolve and in their openness and receptivity
they create a sexual vocabulary and language. They each
bring a different psychology and a different physicality to
that creative act and their private sexuality is shaped by the
effects of gender conditioning in both trivial and fundamental ways.

Eleanor and Jim were both raised according to the
traditional notions of femininity and masculinity. We have
seen how Eleanor had imposed on her by society a split

about female sexuality. She was brought up to know that her sexuality was highly valued and potentially dangerous and that it needed protecting. Inside, she felt somewhat distanced from these two images of herself as either a virgin princess or a dangerous temptress. She did however feel confined by them and was relieved that she could entrust herself to Jim. When she married she really did not know very much about her body from a sexual point of view. Discouraged from exploring 'down there' as a child, learning to be modest about periods, she entered married life as a sexual innocent. She had what was considered a 'good figure', and this contributed to her feelings of self-esteem. But the theme of alienation was perpetuated in this, for, while she knew that her figure was an asset that helped her attract and hold Jim, she knew also that it was not the real her. He was very complimentary about her large breasts and Eleanor saw her body and her sexuality as something that she was giving to him. In sexuality as in other aspects of her development Eleanor had learned to be attentive and giving, putting the needs of the other person first and obscuring the vision of her own needs. She was eager to please Jim and wanted to be a good lover for him. Although she would have described the pleasure in early sexual life together as mutual, at another level we can see that her pleasure depended on giving Jim satisfaction. This situation is reflected in other aspects of being subjected to feminine socialization. Just as Margaret (in Chapter 2) was meant to gain her satisfaction in life from identifying with her husband's pleasures and accomplishments, so too was Eleanor's sexual pleasure to be funnelled through her husband's. Her focus on him was not especially unusual, particularly in the early stage of their marriage. Her mother had indicated to her that the sexual side of marriage was not really such a pleasure for a woman and Eleanor was pleasantly surprised by how much she did enjoy it and how important it was to her. But she was dependent on Jim to introduce her to her own body and its sexual potential. She could not initiate lovemaking — it would never have

occurred to her. She wasn't passive in bed but a part of her
was outside the experience, looking on, making sure that
Jim was as delighted as he could be. She would gladly try
anything Jim proposed and felt contented and good inside
that she was able to make him happy. She liked intercourse
although she was not orgasmic. When Jim entered her she
knew that their lovemaking would finish shortly. She put her
whole body and soul into this part of the lovemaking,
holding him tight, stroking him as she knew he liked. She
purred contentedly when he came and felt satisfied and
warm. His desires framed their lovemaking. She would fix
dinner and set a romantic table, she would wear clothes that
she knew Jim found particularly sexy. She made the sexual
environment in which Jim would act and then she felt good
when he made advances towards her, for she felt that he
very much wanted her and needed her in that way. In their
sexual relationship Eleanor was able to internalize desire
and feel that she was very much a wanted person. She felt
his desire for her and this made her feel good. This also
modified the common experience that we have noticed in
girls: the psychological consequence of being raised as a
second-class citizen is the sense that one is not really wanted
or valued. Eleanor felt valued and appreciated because Jim
would pursue her and pay her a lot of attention and
compliments.

For his part, Jim brought equally stereotyped male
attitudes into his lovemaking with Eleanor. He was very
pleased that he had such a sexy wife. Eleanor was everything
Jim had dreamed or fantasized about. She was warm, open,
receptive and beautiful. He loved her soft body and would
look forward to being enveloped by her. She liked to make
love often and never refused him. She obviously enjoyed
herself and that pleased Jim. He was never nervous
approaching her and he never had difficulty having or
sustaining an erection. Like many men Jim couldn't quite
put into words the profound contentment that making love
gave him. He felt it deeply, but he spoke of it — to his
friends, that is — in terms of accomplishment. He took pride

in knowing that he could satisfy Eleanor. But could he or did he? Unbeknownst to either of them, Eleanor and Jim were involved in a complicated series of sexual transactions and communications that detracted from their potential pleasure. This came to have rather disastrous results in the long term, as we shall explain later in this chapter.

Obviously men and women approach and experience their sexuality and their sexual relationships from very different positions. Their bodies are different and they have been brought up to relate to them differently. Boys' urinary tracts (urethras) are external; they come to handle their penises from a very early age. Their sexual organ is a fact of their daily experience. Along with developing an ease with holding their penises to direct the flow of urine, they *see* themselves being able to. This experience of early mastery feeds the culturally created phenomenon whereby the penis is idolized — power and majesty become associated with the male organ. This notion extends to the male body and boys are encouraged to develop their physical strength and prowess. A young man who is not athletic may feel himself to be unmanly, or perhaps even a weakling. A man is encouraged to use his body as expressive of his power and presence. By contrast a woman's sexual organs are hidden from view; she learns little about them and is not encouraged to take pride in them. But, paradoxically, at the same time there is a great stake on a woman being attractive and being able to reflect the current trends in body size and body image. Women tend to be plagued much more than men with confusion about their body image and this is in part because of the strong emphasis on looking the right way, wearing the right clothes, having the right size breasts for this year's image, having the right kind of hair to fit in. It is as though a woman has to put to one side who she is (sexually and physically) and model herself on the images of femininity that adorn the billboards, magazines, newspapers and TV screens. She then puts on this image as best she can and, alienated from her own body, goes in search of a partner, hoping that she has been able to make herself

sufficiently attractive to interest a man of her choosing. All
women come to feel that their bodies need improving in
some way or another. A woman may dislike her nose, or feel
her legs are too short. She may feel her thighs are too bulky
or her breasts too large or small. She may feel her tummy
sticks out too much or that her muscle tone is no good and so
on. In other words, it is hard to meet a woman who doesn't
feel that there is some physical aspect of her that she would
like to change. The paradox lies in the fact that at the same
time as the woman is trying to make herself as pleasing, and
as sexually attractive, to others as possible, she has been
discouraged from exploring her own body and sexual
organs.

A woman approaches her first sexual relationships, then,
with a certain unease about her body. This may become
focused on being concerned about whether he will enjoy her
body when she takes off her clothes, but this worry often
masks much deeper concerns of whether she will be
accepted and whether she will be able to relax sexually.
When a woman first goes to bed with a man she is looking
for a good sexual experience as well as hoping that here
in this relationship she will gain love, attention, and the
feeling of being wanted and accepted. But deep inside, as
we have seen, she does not expect that her needs will be met.

Two factors inform this expectation. The first is that she
herself does not necessarily know what she wants sexually,
as she has come to have a disjointed relationship with her
body. Until quite recently, for example, many women did
not know about the source of their sexual pleasure. Since
Freud and until Masters and Johnson, the clitoris, the female
equivalent of the penis, was devalued and dismissed. A lot
of hocus-pocus was written in both technical and popular
sexual manuals directing husbands to vaginal stimulation in
order to prepare their wives for penetration. The vulva[3] and
the clitoris, if mentioned, were seen as the site of the

3.   Our thanks to Dr Harriet Lerner for discussion on the role of the vulva
     in women's sexuality.

immature woman's sexual response. The reader was reassured that, to give a woman sexual pleasure, a romantic
atmosphere and a prolonged period of foreplay followed by
intercourse would do the trick. Implicit in these instructions
was the idea that female sexuality was indeed different, for
women needed an emotional atmosphere and a prolonged,
i.e. overlong, stimulation (as though what men needed was
the norm). Women reading these books couldn't help but
pick up the message that a man was doing her a favour, that
his sexual needs were more straightforward and compact,
that there was something special, a bit awkward and fiddly,
about female sexuality. In this as in other aspects of women's
needs, women may come to feel that their desires and wants
are a bit too much. They may feel guilty and awkward if, for
example, oral sex pleases them and brings them to orgasm.
They may fear that it is taking altogether too long and that
their man will lose interest or be bored. They may be so
concerned with their partner's thoughts and feelings and so
disbelieving that they are truly interested and eager to give
that they cannot take in and enjoy what is being given —
*they are hurrying to relieve their partners of the burden of
having to give to them.* Women try to escape from this
because, unaccustomed as they are to getting, when they *do*
receive this kind of love and attention, such an experience
touches off their desires for more of it, at the same time as
they may feel shame about wanting and disbelief that
someone is giving to them.

The second reason why, deep down, a woman may not
expect satisfaction is that she is likely to be far too preoccupied with giving to her partner sexually to make known
to herself and to him what would most please her. She may
well have read and believed that the most legitimate
expression of heterosexual love was intercourse and sim-
ultaneous orgasm. And so she endeavoured to make this
happen. Because she so wants her partner to be happy and
indeed feels her own happiness through his, she applies the
same kind of attentiveness to detail in lovemaking that she
does in intuiting his emotional needs. She conveys to him

that he should let her know what he wants, she makes an environment in which his needs are welcomed.

A woman then is afflicted in the following ways when she enters her first heterosexual relationships: she is distanced from her body, sometimes ignorant about its sexual potential, preoccupied with her partner's experience and unused to receiving.

When a man starts up a sexual relationship he may also be somewhat uneasy. He too is distanced from his sexuality. He approaches sex as though it were a challenge. Giving a woman sexual satisfaction becomes the goal. But the accomplishment is propelled less by altruistic motives and more by needs which actually prevent him from really getting to know a woman's sexuality. There is no such thing as one view of female sexuality. For him, female sexuality is a conglomerate of the myriad of images displayed before him daily. Women's sexuality seems to be all around him and yet untouchable. Women's bodies sell him everything from soap to cars. Women are seducers as well as the prize. He has to juggle pictures of movie star goddesses, the women in his everyday life and his fantasies when choosing a lover. His sexuality is seen as more physical than emotional although sexual encounters for him fulfil very important needs.

A man very much wants to please a woman sexually. But as we have seen, men looking to learn from sex manuals or from other men by and large find information which is inadequate, for it reflects *men's* ideas about women's sexuality rather than detailing women's actual experience of sex. Joe, a writer now in his thirties and living happily with Valerie, recalls, 'When I was in my late teens and twenties the whole sex business was really touch and go for me. I knew the most important thing was to make a girl come and I was always worried that I wouldn't be able to keep going long enough to satisfy her. My basic knowledge was simply this. You spent a lot of time juicing a woman up — just till you thought she was about to come, mainly you did this by making sure she was wet and touching around the general vaginal area, hoping you were doing it right — and then, when I thought she was ready, I would enter her and hope that I wouldn't come right away. In one way I was very involved with giving her pleasure, but in another way I see now that I didn't have a clue about what I was doing. I felt really good if I thought she was satisfied and here's the crazy part, not because it made her especially happy, at least it didn't seem to, but because I felt manly. I suppose now I see it as a bit self-involved and like a test. If she came, my self-esteem rose. It wasn't too much about showing love, it was more about achieving some difficult feat.' He went on, 'It wasn't until Valerie and I got together that I got a whole new perspective on it and had to face that probably all that macho business didn't add up to much. One of the main things I think now is, I was so concerned about doing it right I never stopped to ask or to find out if it was really nice for *her*.' Joe was a victim, like so many men then, to mis-information on the one hand and a macho self-image on the other. He was caught up in proving his sexual prowess to himself to an extent that prevented him from really being much more than a technician rather than the lover he wanted to be. He hid his vulnerability and his anxieties behind an image of virility. In fact he wasn't even aware at the time that he was tense or insecure because his sexually eager and capable image worked fairly successfully for him.

So we can see how the unequal exchange between women's and men's needs plays out in the sexual arena. A woman is preoccupied with a man's needs because that is where she has learned to spend her attention. Her dis-comfort with her own sexual needs and her body, and her disbelief that anyone will give to her or be there for her, prevent her from articulating her desires. The man mean-while is frequently unaware of really how ignorant he is about female sexuality. He assumes he knows what is going on and what a woman wants because his upbringing has given him a basic sense that what he knows is, is. His vulnerabilities are locked behind layers and layers of socialization so that he can't easily bring them out into the open, examine them and engage with them. Both people are working on fragile premises, the woman always thinking others know best, which isn't of course true; the man thinking he knows best, which is equally untrue.

Rosemary and Neil's relationship (see Chapter 4) shows another facet of what sexuality is meant to convey. Although they had been living together for ten years, Rosemary was terribly insecure. Neil could never tell her that he loved her and Rosemary lived with the constant worry that he would leave her for someone else. She stayed with him because she loved him, always hoped things would change, and that he would be more open — as indeed he was when he relaxed by getting drunk or smoking pot. Rosemary was sexually inexperienced when she met Neil. He was her first lover and she was very happy to be involved with him. Although Neil had not had that many girlfriends, he projected an aura of confidence and experience in sexual matters — especially as compared to Rosemary. Rosemary saw Neil as much more knowledgeable about sex than she and relied on him to take the initiative both as to when they would make love and how they made love. As the relationship continued, their love-making became more and more infrequent. Rosemary made attempts to revive their sex life but Neil did not respond to her advances and was a bit disdainful. Rosemary in turn felt hurt and rejected and gave up trying to initiate things even though she wanted to make love. She waited instead for his infrequent urges.

The actual quality of their lovemaking was not splendid but Rosemary longed for the physical contact, the hugging, stroking and holding that was part of it. Beyond that, though, the sexual encounters had symbolic significance. Rosemary desperately wanted acceptance and reassurance that Neil loved her and this longing was transferred into craving symbols of acceptance such as having regular sex. It was less important to her what transpired in the sexual encounter; what was important was that it showed her she was wanted. Neil would get incensed with her if she asked him to show his commitment directly, shouting, 'Isn't living with you proof enough that I care!' He made Rosemary feel crazy that she was wanting too much. And because Rosemary was always showing how much she wanted and needed him, he never had to confront his own needs for her. We can see the cha-cha dynamic in their sexual relationship. The more she wanted, the more he backed off. When she was able to be caught up in her work life and not so apparently interested in or in need of him, Neil would approach her sexually. In actual fact, Neil was afraid and uncomfortable with his own sexuality and he was somewhat scared of Rosemary's. Before Rosemary he had gone out with a few women but had never formed a close attachment. Women's sexuality seemed to him very mysterious and powerful.

However, for Neil, intercourse itself was always wonderful. He described it as being totally at ease and exhilarated at the same time. He felt good, warm, and content. He felt accepted and whole at a very deep level. It felt like losing consciousness and at the same time being terribly alive. He felt merged with Rosemary as though they were one.

After lovemaking, however, he would feel incredibly depressed and let down. He didn't really know why, because moments before he had felt so very close to her. He would want to go off by himself or turn over and go to sleep, to separate himself from Rosemary, to shake her out of him. As we examined this desire and his avoidance of sex between the two of them, it turned out that he was terrified by having such strong feelings with a woman. It made him feel vulnerable, a bit helpless as though he was losing power and control. He couldn't bear to be in a woman's power — as he saw it — even though the sexual experience was so ecstatic for him. It scared him to feel so close that he was merged. In therapy he came to realize that avoiding intercourse was just one way in which his fear of being close to Rosemary showed itself. He realized that he often did not satisfy Rosemary sexually but kept her dangling. As long as she was vaguely unsatisfied, Rosemary was clingy, always wanting some form of contact with Neil. Although Neil disliked that part of Rosemary, it served a purpose; it allowed him to see her as the dependent one in the relationship. Rosemary pointed out that whenever she did feel sexually satisfied she was aware of a different quality in her attachment to Neil. She felt as though she wasn't looking to him for reassurance all the time but was feeling contented and at peace with herself. She didn't feel she was desperately seeking involvement or contact. When he was rejecting or distant, and she couldn't rely on their sexual encounters to get close, she felt cast out and anxious. She pursued him but projected a worry that she would be turned away.

This fear of the merger that Neil expressed is felt by women, too. For in lovemaking especially, where two people feel very close, the physical and emotional pleasure that they can create together often touches off echoes of our very earliest experiences in the world when we were merged with our mothers. In this original merger our world was essentially sensual. In it, we experienced bliss and terrible discomfort. We could not control these feelings. We could only hope that mother knew when we were hungry or could tell when our nappies were cold and wet. We were suspended in a physical world without the physical strength to make things happen for us. Sex can remind us of the vulnerability that our physical smallness and immaturity aroused, and the echo of the merger with mother re-evokes our struggle in trying to differentiate from her, to be different, to separate ourselves psychologically, to need her less. In sex, we are plunged once again into a world awash with physical, sensual expression. We lose the studied and conscious sense of ourselves. Our physical and emotional armour temporarily dissolves and we melt into an experience of oneness. We find the mate, the partner we've longed for. We are each reunited with the warming, accepting aspects of mother. We long to be engulfed, surrounded and enclosed in a physical-emotional orbit. In heterosexual love, men make a symbolic re-entry into that mysterious, soft, all-embracing world. For a woman the (usually) larger body of the man holding her symbolizes that original merger. These resonances with the infant state before separation-individuation arouse in all of us complicated reactions, as we have already seen. At the same time that we can give ourselves up to the embrace of that psycho-physical state, we wish to escape it. For when we feel so close to another person that the physical boundaries between us have been crossed, we may feel the precariousness of our psychological boundaries. We play out an adult version of the struggle to separate from mother. We may be scared by our loved one's ability to get under our skin. We may run from the recognition of our urgent need to be involved. We may try to shake off the depth of our adult involvement by denying our dependency and need for another. We both yearn for and are wary of the quality of that early infantile dependency.

The dissolving of the psycho-physical boundaries that occurs in heterosexual love can be even more pronounced between two women. Gillian and Rose had both been sexually involved with men before they became lovers. In fact, when they first started sleeping together, Rose was still living with and having occasional sex with her husband. Both of them were enthralled by their love affair and by the ways in which they approached sex together. It was so different from the heterosexual circumstances they were used to. They both felt shy and vulnerable but at the same time relaxed and responsive. Neither of them felt they had to show each other the way or be the one in control. They could learn together what pleased them and they felt free of an internal pressure to hurry up. They were comfortable exploring the delights of each other's bodies, at once so similar and so different. They both felt more involved and swept up in this relationship than ever before and were able, because of loving each other's bodies, to allow that acceptance of femininity to reflect in themselves. They both noticed a new appreciation of their own bodies which accompanied a drop in the level of their preoccupation with the 'faults' of their physical appearance. They were

enormously happy sexually. They didn't hesitate to find out
what pleased each other, and they were both good givers.
The only perplexing aspect of their sexual relationship was
what followed immediately after sex. It was as though they
went through a process in which they had to make a point of
physically disengaging. One of them, usually Rose, would
jump out of bed, and spend ages in the shower. At first
Gillian was very hurt by this but then she appreciated being
on her own for a bit. They both noticed this physical
distancing and neither of them knew exactly what was going
on. Rose thought that perhaps she felt guilty that the lovemaking was so good and that like many people having
clandestine affairs she was trying to wash Gillian out of her
system. But this explanation didn't make nearly as much
sense to her as the visual picture she had of their entwine-
ment and the absolute contentment it aroused in her. What
they both realized was that they had been so merged during
the lovemaking, and so very taken up in it and by it, that they
really didn't feel a sense of their own physical boundaries.
Having a brief separation right after lovemaking pulled
them back into themselves. Their merger touched off fears
in both of them that they would be stuck together, lose their
own identity and be subsumed by the other.

As we have seen, the process of girls separating from their
mother is a difficult one. The mother, because of her shared
gender, relates to her daughter as though she were an
extension of herself. This makes it hard for the daughter to
know herself apart from her mother. On top of this, the
mother has often not been able to give steady nurturing to
her daughter because of the push-pull dynamic. As we saw
with Katie in Chapter 2, and with so many of the women we
have met on these pages, the daughter then moves away
from her mother with trepidation, not terribly sure of her
own boundaries, feeling somewhat insecure and shaky about
her sense of self as different from her mother. When two
women open themselves up to each other in a close sexual
relationship, they may both be touched by echoes of that
early merger with mother. They may both long to be

reunited now in this adult way with a warm, soft, loving, accepting woman. They may be overwhelmed by how much pleasure they experience and by how easily their boundaries dissolve and they feel the possibility of merger.

When boys are separating from their mother, they and the mother use the fact of their gender difference in that process. Boys rely on these differences in the creating of boundaries that then help them differentiate psychologically.[4] (They may live much more rigidly behind these boundaries on a day-to-day basis and approach situations and relationships with what appears to be a clear sense of self, even if the origin of this sense of self is arrived at in its own way somewhat precariously, i.e. in opposition or defensively.) The development of a masculine psychology has at its roots the need to differentiate and separate from a woman. This poses psychological problems for men when they get close to a woman. They unconsciously fear a loss not just of a separate identity but of their masculine identity. They may perceive the echoes in the merger in intercourse as a regression, and fear re-incorporation with their mother. This unconscious fantasy prevents many men from getting close or sustaining the intimacy that is in their heterosexual relationship.

The fear of the loss of masculinity from the merger is but one side of a precarious sense of masculinity wrought by our conditioning system. The overvaluation of the penis, the visible manifestation that the son is indeed different from the mother, arises in part out of a need to demythologize the mother and hence all women. A male organ is used to produce real boundaries, and is then invested with the power to 'do' things to women. A man's penis becomes for him a symbol of his power and control over women, but it has another more hidden function. It is for him a crucial reassurance of his separateness and difference from first his mother, and later all women. The sense of masculinity rests on a notion, perhaps a buried one, of males as other,

4.   R. Stoller, *Sex and Gender*, London 1969.

different, not like females. It is ironic that this very sense of other has found a cultural translation in patriarchy in the exclusion of women from political, economic, social, sexual or legal equity, so that it is the woman who becomes and carries the emotional burden of being the outsider, the other. A man's holding on to his penis as the centre of his being and as an instrument for control and power over women represents another way in which men's fear of facing their dependency needs adds to difficulties in the bedroom.

Men and women are fearful of female sexuality. The very idea of it is so threatening that, even now, a woman in her twenties to forties who is not attached to a man may be desexualized as the spinster or oversexualized as the nymphomaniac. A middle-aged woman interested in sex can still be the object of embarrassment; a young divorcee or widow seems to ignite sexual fears and fantasies in a well-established social group. Female sexuality is mysterious, unknowable, and must be contained. Here's Johnny reflecting on the impact of his upbringing: 'I think men grow up to feel that we were always supposed to be ready for sex and that women were really reluctant. The sexpots in the movies contradicted the idea, but they only existed on celluloid, which was a relief, because god knows what I would have done with a real Ava Gardner. I was supposed to be able to turn a woman on, drive her out of her mind, and all the time stay on top of the situation myself. Once I was involved with a woman, Anne, who was totally wild sexually. She just gave herself up to the situation. It was great but pretty hairy there for a while because I was worried that I couldn't meet her excitement. I could feel a bit left out and overwhelmed and out of control. I think I feel easier when a woman matches my excitement. If she surpasses it in a way that I notice, I feel like there's a demand on me I might not know how to meet.'

Johnny talked about how not being in control affected him in two ways. He felt potentially inadequate and that he could lose the self-esteem he derived from 'satisfying a woman'. If a woman was very keen on sex, and he wasn't responsible for making the best use of her sexual potential, managing her sexuality by pushing the right buttons and controlling what happened when he did, then in a strange way he felt the woman would not need him and would be separate. 'For me it's a question of her not being involved in the sex for me but for herself. This makes me angry, I feel neglected. I can feel that she's abandoned me. It's one thing if I give her an orgasm and she's being nice to me by accepting it. It's another if she's in there for herself.' When Johnny was involved with Anne, the siren, he was scared about losing her all the time. When she left the apartment in the morning looking smashing, he would feel annoyed that she was showing the world her sexuality. Her display made him feel insecure and uneasy. He couldn't stand it and they broke off when in a fight he called her a 'whore'.

Johnny drifted from his relationship into a series of one-night stands and casual encounters. In these liaisons, he was searching for instant contact without much involvement. His self-esteem was at a low point and he sought out women in singles bars hoping to be taken home by one of them. The women he was attracted to all seemed to be eager for a secure relationship rather than the casual sex he was looking for. He found himself sleeping with several different women, feeling close during sex, but with little desire to pursue a relationship. He wasn't really ready to get involved with anyone and he sought the sexual encounters as a substitute for relating. The various women would listen to his problems, try to soothe away his upset and offer him a warm and sensual body to lie with through the night. He was able to get the benefits of women's nurturing skills at a point when he was feeling vulnerable and shaky, without making a commitment he wasn't ready for.

Sheila, a twenty-eight year old assistant record producer who hung out in singles bars, was clear that she was only looking for one-night stands too. In these encounters she sought confirmation that she was attractive and could interest a man. She did not expect tenderness or an especially receptive ear (she relied on her girlfriends for these things). She was proving to herself that she was appealing. At the bar she was quite forward in going after the men she wanted. She enjoyed being able to choose and be active rather than wait for the men to pick her out. About twice a week she took a new man home with her although she didn't let anyone spend the whole night with her. She was involved in a struggle between the two different parts of herself. One part of her desperately wanted to be involved in a sexual relationship and another part of her didn't. Of course the situation was not as straightforward as that. Sheila despaired of ever meeting anyone she would really like and trust. She had been badly hurt by Fred when he unexpectedly left her for a man. Fred had been very emotionally present and warm. Not dazzling sexually, but certainly attentive and she had felt very close to him. Although she had later learned that he had always been more attracted to men and his decision to break up with her and get involved with Bob had been an agonizing one for him, she couldn't help translate his homosexuality as a rejection of her. In her two-evenings-a-week ritual she was constantly involved in testing out her attractiveness and, once having reassured herself that she could indeed attract the men that appealed to her, she would lose interest in them. Each encounter expressed both the love she wanted and at the same time reaffirmed its impossibility. Sheila and Johnny both used sex in order to be in the rejecting role. They both derived boosts to their self-esteem in the process. Johnny would find attentive, solicitous women. Sheila got a constant confirmation of her sex appeal and attractiveness. She was trying to undo the rejection of her femininity that she experienced with Fred. For both of them, one-night stands were a way to have warmth and contact within safely prescribed boundaries in which their dependency needs did not leak out more than either of them could handle. They both felt good on the surface that they didn't need to be in a lasting relationship.

The search for a partner in life, someone with whom to share and create a personal world, is shaped by a complex of

factors. For many couples the sexual aspect of the relationship is a dynamic force from the beginning even if, like
Eleanor and Jim, they did not have intercourse for several
years. Sexual attraction between two people is an important
binder, and curiously this is so whether or not the sex is
satisfactory. In choosing a partner, we are first drawn to the
physical presence of another, how they hold themselves,
what they project about themselves, what they are wearing, how they move their bodies and so on. We may be
physically attracted to someone who, when we get to know
them, does not fulfil our expectations and so the sexual
attraction evaporates. Our capacity to respond is connected
with the concept of relating, getting physically close to
another. Even in a zipless fuck we seek an intense connection. The desire for physical expression and release
occurs in all relationships, however transitory.

Our sexual desire can be stimulated by the shape of a
hand, the wiggle of a hip, the look in someone's eyes. Any
part of the body can become an area that another finds
erotic. When we are sexually attracted to someone, con-
juring up a picture of how they look can spark off gentle
sexual feelings. Many people feel this way about their
partners ten, fifteen, or twenty years after living with and
having sex with them. Deidre was married to David for
eighteen years. She would look at him sitting and reading
across the room, and feel warm and melty inside. These
feelings did not carry over to the bedroom, however. They
made love regularly and it was physically enjoyable, but she
could hardly remember the last time she felt passionate or
full of desire. She missed the urgency of their early lovemaking and wondered how something once so pressing had
become routine and pedestrian.

We have heard this complaint so often that we are bound
to ask what happens to sexual ardour in a long-term relationship. Why does the passion in so many relationships get
tamed? Why is there so frequently a downward spiral of
interest and deep enjoyment? How does being emotionally
dependent and more or less secure affect the texture of our

sexual relationships? Of course not all sexual relationships provide less satisfaction or deteriorate over time, but so many do, and so many people have the experience of being sexually dulled, or of going to bed night after night knowing that sex is not on the agenda.

Some of the reasons are fairly obvious. As couples spend more time with each other and are involved in the process of sharing a life together, sexuality is not the exclusive area for the expression of close personal intimacy. Living together also involves things like cooking together, chatting cosily by the fire, taking walks, doing domestic chores. These activities all become vehicles for sharing and take on their particular meaning in the life of the couple. For Saul and Jane, cooking together was not only a sensual pleasure, it was a creative expression of their involvement with each other. They worked together in the kitchen almost wordlessly, Saul stirring Jane's pot, Jane adding seasoning to a dish Saul started. They communicated without speaking and they trusted each other completely, enjoying the innovations and building on the repertoire each brought to the marriage. They harmonized beautifully in the kitchen and never once had a row. They enjoyed the whole process from cooking to eating together, it was a shared intimate experience. The energy originally riveted on the sexual aspects of their relating was now somewhat diverted into cooking and other activities. They both wondered why their sex wasn't so passionate but they weren't aware of being dissatisfied with each other.

When a couple falls in love, the reality of the outside world is temporarily pushed back by the intensity of the emotional nesting. But soon, and only slowly at first, the couple has to come to grips with their relationship as a part of the world. As the couple 'hatches', so the magically intense membrane in which it lives dissolves. Each member of the couple introduces the other into their world. The integration of the one person into another's life has the effect of narrowing the distance between private life and the public world. As these worlds become more interwoven there may be an impact on sexual communications. This, the most private of communications, may change ever so slightly. It may no longer be as special, as separate, as preserved or as protected as it was before. Like eating together, it takes on a variety of meanings. Sometimes it is romantic and extraordinary; often it is approached unthinkingly out of habit; sometimes it is a desire on the part of one member of the couple that the other is happy to respond to but isn't inspired by. The ordinary weariness of life seeps into all of our activities. Sex and love, then, stay protected in the bubble for only a relatively short time span.

Living together for several years can result in 'taking each other for granted'. This can produce positive and/or negative effects. On the positive side, taking one's partner for granted may occur because one is able to rely on their being there. Secure in the relationship, one is not constantly caught up in worrying about being left or deserted. But one may also 'take a partner for granted' because one has stopped relating directly. The couple may have become so enmeshed in the transference aspects of the relationship that they are not really aware of who the other person actually is and what their needs are. For example, if each partner is carrying a mother transference towards the other, they may each imagine that the other is not as attentive or responsive as they might be at the same time as believing the other will never leave them. This negative aspect of 'taking for granted' exacts its toll in the bedroom. For, because one may be unaware of the other person's needs in the relationship, a real distance builds up which the sexual encounter cannot necessarily bridge in a truly satisfying way. The sex is based on each person's ideal of who the other is rather than a shared knowledge and intimacy. Hoping that sex *can* bridge the distance inevitably leads to disappointment, and unsatisfying sex does not build an appetite for more. The couple try to reach each other through sex, but fail.

When each partner takes the other for granted, the relationship freezes. The transactions and communications are hedged in by fear and innuendo. Each partner 'knows'

what upsets the other and often stays away from discussing
it, scared to tip the equilibrium that has been established.
Certain topics may become taboo or at least difficult to
explore and so a rigidity develops. Not only is each partner
not really seen, they can begin to conform to the picture the
other holds, by not bringing certain aspects of themselves
into the relationship. This dynamic not only affects the
sexual relationship, it also occurs within it. In many, many
couples with whom we have talked and counselled, there is a
fear, which then translates into an unwillingness to expose
their needs sexually and find out each other's. For example,
consider Eleanor and Jim, the couple who had married in
the late '50s when the sexual mores and knowledge about
female sexual response were different from what they are
today. About four years into their sexual relationship, as
Eleanor came to know her body better, her sexual desires
changed and she very much wanted to be stimulated orally.
Once, when she and Jim had oral sex, she experienced her
first orgasm. She was somewhat ashamed of this because she
felt that it should have occurred during intercourse. After
the first orgasm, she began to masturbate on her own but she
felt very guilty about it. She felt that Jim should be giving her
that kind of pleasure, rather than herself, and that ideally she
should be able to come when he had his orgasm during
intercourse. As she was able to satisfy herself, she became
less fully 'present' when she had sex with Jim and very
confused about the situation. Jim felt something had
changed slightly but didn't know what and didn't want to
pressure her. They got into a routine of making love a couple
of times a week, but looking back on it now she realized the
sex between them was a disappointment. For, on Jim's part,
her withdrawal made him feel less relaxed and open himself.
Except on rare occasions, their lovemaking became routine
and less and less passionate for both of them. They took each
other's moves for granted, and could predict the course of
feelings that would transpire for both of them. Eleanor
meanwhile felt guilty and Jim started to develop quite active
fantasies of what he would like to be going on in bed.

Eleanor could not overcome her prejudiced ideas about intercourse being 'the real thing' and could not bring herself to tell Jim what she wanted. He didn't know what was going on in her mind and he was unable to ask her if she needed something to change in the lovemaking. He was also scared to show her that something was missing for him. He felt a bit ashamed of his fantasies and didn't know how to tell her about them. The passion got tamed then, because neither of them could really talk about this non-verbal activity easily. They settled for minimum sexual involvement as they weren't able to look at what was going on between them for many, many years. The couple counselling made it easier for Eleanor and Jim to talk about their sexual relationship. Eleanor was able to tell him what she enjoyed and he was relieved to have this information and to know what had been going on. Jim now felt delighted to integrate Eleanor's pleasures into their lovemaking. The spoken communications opened up their sexual relationship and they approached it again with vigour and excitement.

Talking about the change in regularity of sexual relations, in the quality of those relations and in the long-term interest in them seems to be an extremely charged issue for many people. This in itself already tells us something, for the very fact that people are uncomfortable about looking at their sex lives indicates a certain unease, a disappointment, a shame that things aren't as they should be.

Often one partner in a couple has a misperception about the other's level of satisfaction or dissatisfaction. There may be a sexual cha-cha going on that isn't even acknowledged, for individuals perceive needs differently. But the fact that someone who, as we have seen, is so finely tuned at an emotional level to the ups and downs of the relationship, to the mood of the other, can be so oblivious to their partner's sexual dissatisfaction is itself extremely revealing. Women and men come to sex with different expectations and different needs. For example, men look to sex to affirm their identity. In lovemaking they assert their masculinity and it is powerfully reflected back to them. It bolsters their male

identity which is less stable than might at first appear.
Women often trade sex as though it were a commodity in
their search for security, warmth, affection, love, and economic protection. Women approach sex looking for connection. Men come to it for contact too but also to confirm
their difference. These unconscious threads that propel our
sexual encounters mean that, at least on this level, men and
women are not meeting in the bedroom but are looking for
very different things which neither of them know about. A
partner's perception that he or she isn't having enough sex,
and the partner's sense that they are, then relates to these
different needs.

So far we have established how sex-role education
prepares and un-prepares each of us for the bedroom. But in
all intimate relationships, as we have seen, there is both the
current person that each partner is relating to and the
transference overlays that affect our perceptions of our
partners, our hopes of who they can be for us, our
projections and our disappointments.

If we remember the psychological picture we have drawn
of women and men, we recall that at each developmental
stage, beginning with the texture of that first early dependency on the caretaking mother, the way girls and boys are
related to is based on their gender. Their passage from that
early dependency to separation-individuation structures
their psyches in gender-linked ways. Girls' shared gender
with mother and the social meaning of that similarity in
patriarchy creates the push-pull dynamic in the mother-
daughter relationship. This means that girls often don't
receive enough nurturance to separate from the relationship
with their mother. The attempt to separate and become
one's own person is extremely fraught. And consequently, as
we have seen, girls grow up feeling needy, perplexed as to
why they are inconsistently related to, internalize the rejection, feel ashamed of the desire to be cared for emotionally
and are in an unconscious search for a mother who will make
it better. Women bring these longings to their sexual
relationships whether these are with men or with women.

Boys' separation from mother is also fraught. Mothers have complex conscious and unconscious feelings about raising sons in patriarchy, and this is reflected in the kinds of relating between a mother and son. The son may be the recipient of mother's (and father's) idealization at one moment as the little prince, and at another he may suffer the effects of her unconscious rage, envy and contempt for the meaning of being male in our society. When boys try to separate from mother, they may also not have received sufficient nurture — although the expectation of getting stays with them. More importantly for its implications in terms of male-female sexual relationships, the boy in distinguishing himself is involved in a process of disidentification from the feminine aspects of himself that he has internalized, and attempts to distance himself from the mother whose emotional world has held him. He is helped to suppress these aspects of self in the passage through boyhood to manhood and these important parts of himself are compartmentalized, sometimes so deeply hidden that the man knows nothing about them, or they may emerge in extremely upsetting ways as was the case with Neil. For most men, though, this part of them is encouraged to come out the most in the intimacy of their sexual relationship. Particularly in heterosexual relationships, women work hard to create an atmosphere in which the man will feel comfortable enough to bare his soul, show his insides, expose his vulnerabilities and the tenderer side of his personality.

Just as women are involved in an unconscious search for a mother in life who will love them unconditionally, so too do men want the kind of attentiveness, nurturance and caring that we associate with mothering. In heterosexual love, both partners may experience a temporary loss of psycho-physical boundaries, and in the merger transferences may be occurring in which *each* partner is also reunited with the longed-for mother. This aspect of a sexual relationship can, as we saw with Neil and Rosemary or Gillian and Rose, be experienced as frightening, for it exposes the longing, the desire to collapse, to experience as an adult the holding embrace of a safe womb. However, transference within a close relationship is not always damaging. For the experience of being temporarily merged and satisfied in that merger can contribute to a person's sense of well-being when they reintegrate back into themselves. In falling in love and in having sex, there are many unconscious factors that lie beneath the surface that motivate us in ways that once examined would seem to have little to do with 'healthy', loving impulses. But in falling in love and in lovemaking, there is a process of repair to the low self-esteem and sense of self that so many people suffer. For *being loved* allows one to see and experience oneself differently. One is taking in the love that another is giving (even if they may be in part giving out of narcissistic needs). This love can enter into the well of longing or the emptiness that lives deep inside us. It can feed us in profoundly important ways and transform deeply held images of unconnectedness. The change that it can produce internally may then change the shape of what each partner is wanting and needing in the sexual relationship. Love may be able to divest itself of the driven aspects of narcissistic relating. Close lovemaking and being loved may help two people experience a sense of self sufficient to begin to relate out of a new wholeness rather than out of a desperate need to fill the void. The connection is now rephrased. This phenomenon occurred in Eleanor and Jim's relationship. Of course there were other factors that contributed to their sexuality being less intense on a regular basis, but part of the shift was to do with their coming to feel, through love, very different about themselves, very much surer of themselves, and hence not so driven to find a meaning or a context totally in another's life. Their sex became less frenzied then, because its early intensity had contained elements related to issues of transference and narcissistic needs. When these needs were met, the sex no longer became the vehicle or carried them.

On the surface, sexual dependency needs, especially the man's, may not be obvious, but as we look at the sexual relationship, trying to understand how men's and women's needs for contact, nurturance and dependency intersect, a complicated picture unfolds which reveals the paradox that men enjoy sex at the same time as feeling uneasy about exposing their vulnerability and their needs. Women meanwhile often substitute sex and sexuality as a vehicle for the emotional contact they so desperately want and don't find sufficiently in their heterosexual relationships. For both, sex serves as a highly charged symbolic expression of generally inarticulated dependency needs.

6

Pregnancy and Dependency

The decision to have a child is a milestone in the life of a couple. When two people want to have a child together they are making a statement about their feelings for one another. A child represents the merger and intimacy of the couple relationship. Just as the two people have created a relationship and nourished loving feelings between them, they create a new life. Achieving love and intimacy has a sense of movement forward, a working towards something, creating something together, working towards and believing in a future. Reproducing a child together also represents this move forward and the belief in life and growth. The birth of a child represents both the merger of two people as well as the transforming quality of love — that is, just as an intimate relationship allows and demands that a person change and grow, so too does a baby represent transformation, growth, newness, development. Pregnancy sparks off specific issues concerning dependency for the expectant couple. For there is the anticipated dependency of the baby — the realization that infants are vulnerable and need care, attention and love. Mothers and fathers relate to this challenge in gender-linked ways based on conditioning. A mother may worry about whether she can give enough emotionally, while a father may be preoccupied with thoughts about whether he can be a good enough material provider. It takes two to make a baby but, by and large, women raise children, so women have a different relationship with their children from men's. There is an imbalance in the contact, the understanding, the intimacy between mother and child and father and child. The plan to enjoy the child as a mutual experience, a shared experience, is knocked off course because of the child-rearing arrangements which have women as the primary caretakers and men somewhere in the background or off to the side. Women spend the majority of time with the infant; they are responsible for learning to understand the meanings of various cries, they are the ones upon whom the infant depends for its very survival. This new dependency, the dependency of an infant, is so great that it often creates a shift in the dependency dynamic which existed for the couple before the birth of the child.

For many women, the fact of being pregnant brings with it feelings of self-esteem and accomplishment. A woman's feelings that she is experiencing something very special may build her confidence and self-respect. She may change so that she no longer seeks a certain confirmation from her partner.

Other women, however, report feeling more dependent on their partners during pregnancy. They feel a bit more vulnerable and begin to feel the burden of responsibility for this new life inside them. With this new and major responsibility they become more aware of their own need for someone to rely on and trust. Some men find this time rewarding because caring for the woman allows them to feel more a part of the birth process. They enjoy feeling needed in this way. It may be one of the few times when a man can experience his own desire and ability to nurture. Caring for the woman feels at the same time like a direct caring for the baby to come. He cannot feel the life inside his own body and he needs the woman to share her body, to let him be a part of the physical nurturance during pregnancy. Some men have difficulties with the woman's increased dependency during pregnancy. They may unconsciously feel frightened of her need; they may feel inadequate in the situation which they imagine to be awesome; they may feel controlled or trapped by her increasing dependency and the impending dependency of the coming child.

With the birth of the child there obviously is the chance for the man to care directly for the child. He now has direct access and no longer has the frustration of feeling outside the situation.

The existence of a third person, a visibly dependent person, in what previously was a household of two, is a dramatic change. The birth of a child not only alters the emotional environment in which the couple lives, but the child also brings new dimensions to the lives of each parent individually. Each parent must respond in one way or another to the child's dependency needs. Dependency as a theme is squarely on the agenda. This is a time when the couple can renegotiate their own dependency on one another as they develop a relationship to their new child who is utterly dependent on them. In Chapter 8 we address the significance of this shared parenting and its impact on dependency and emotional and psychological life. Because most of us were raised by our mothers (especially in the first year of life) and because this by and large is still the practice in most families today, we describe here the effects of dependency in a family where the mother raises the children.

Because of the asymmetry in women's and men's emotional dependency needs and because women are the caretakers of infants and children we can see a serious flaw in our society's system for raising children. That is because women as mothers often feel emotionally deprived themselves, and because they feel so hungry for emotional nurturance they look to their children to fill this emptiness. This 'unhealthy' dynamic is built into the structure of our society. After all, from the time she was a little girl herself the woman was taught to feel that her fulfilment in life would come when she was a mother. A girl is led to believe that the highlight of her life comes with marriage and then the birth of her children. Her marriage may satisfy her dependency needs to some extent, but more often than not women are disappointed emotionally by marriage. The dreams of finally having someone to love and care for her are somewhat dampened. Even in a happy marriage the woman's search for equal emotional exchange, acceptance and love falls short. A new infant can make the woman feel pleased and proud that here is the proof that she can produce something of worth — a perfect, beautiful, healthy little baby which came from inside her. The baby immediately becomes a symbol of her self-worth. The baby can be an extension of herself in the world.

As we know, a newborn infant does not yet have a fixed personality — it is not until approximately age two that toddlers assert themselves and fight for their sense of autonomy and independence. In those early months when the baby is developing, it spends all its time with a woman who has come to feel that her baby is her only domain in life — the only person over whom she has some power and control. Psychological theories always blame mothers for all of our neuroses, but that is only an indictment of a society which restricts women from developing other aspects of themselves and their lives, a society that keeps women in the home doing domestic chores and raising children. It is not mothers who are to blame. Mothers do as best as they can do in their social role. It is quite amazing that people turn out as well as they do given the level of deprivation and oppression women experience. Women are angry and depressed, they feel themselves to be empty, unworthy, undeserving and yet they manage to give love and care and protection and nurturance to their infants and children.

A woman may shift some of her dependency on to her children and away from her partner. She becomes involved with her children emotionally in ways which may be more intimate than with her partner. The man, who may have difficulty in feeling close to and relating intimately with his children, is further distanced and removed from the picture. First he is not there as often because he is out at work and then when he is there he still remains an outsider. It is a mutually unsatisfactory situation. Children feel deprived of their fathers and fathers are deprived of their children.

The mother who feels deprived of a certain level of emotional involvement with her partner turns her needs and attentions to her children. Her deprivation together with her social role as mother tend to make her 'over' involved with her children, too attached. We come full circle. The boy child attempts to separate himself from this woman he has been attached to by defining himself as not like her. He represses aspects of himself that he has taken in from her. He separates defensively and constructs psychological boundaries which hide his own femininity and dependency. Unconsciously he comes to feel frightened of women and their power, and this fear he buries in his infantile memories. As a man he comes to feel frightened of women's needs for him because he is scared that he will be taken over and trapped. He remembers his mother needing and holding on to him in certain ways and has difficulty in his mature attachment to a woman.

Girls, on the other hand, have a more difficult time breaking away from their mother's needs and dependency. After all, who better than a daughter to be aware of the needs of someone so close? Mother expects to be looked after by a daughter in a way that she didn't with her son. The daughter has learned not to expect emotional caretaking (after all, mother feels deprived of it and didn't get it) and she learns that she must get it another way — by giving to others. She comes to feel hungry, deprived and frightened of her own 'insatiability', just as her mother felt. She searches for a partner who will meet her need. She finds this person and her needs are satisfied to a certain extent perhaps. She may choose to have children and the wheel of dependency turns once again with a complicated mixture of the woman responding to the needs of her infant at the same time as she sees in the body of her child the infant part of herself which still needs and wants nurturance.

Pete complained to his brother about the lack of sexual activity that he and Laura were having. His brother's wife coincidentally brought up in her conversation with Laura the topic of their sex life. Laura said that she wasn't particularly interested in sex these days but that it wasn't really a problem and that she thought things were fine in that department. In fact, everything wasn't really fine as far as

Laura was concerned and she could no more tell her sister-in-law about it than she could tell Pete. She was upset about her own lack of interest in sex and she had bad feelings about being someone who didn't have an active, joyful sex life. She had always been very interested in lovemaking before her children were born. When she was feeding her first child, she found that all her energy for emotional and physical contact was diverted into that new relationship. When the baby was two and the character of their involvement changed, her interest in Pete reasserted itself strongly, more strongly than they seemed to have time for. But Pete, unbeknownst to Laura, was having an affair with one of his students and was insensitive to or uninterested in her sexual cues. Pete and Laura had become out of sync sexually, as can often happen when a couple have a child. During the baby's first months of life, especially where the mother is doing most of the parenting, most of the mother's attention may be focused on her relationship with the baby. She and the infant live in a different world from the father. If he is scared of the baby and loath to relate actively to it, then the world of mother and baby appears sealed off. Father may lose the attention of his partner as well as be threatened by her involvement with another. Unconsciously oedipal echoes may be re-evoked. As a boy he coped with the dramatic evidence of his mother's involvement with another, when he realized the importance of mother and father's relationship and became for the first time aware that while mother was his first love, mother herself had another involvement. Perhaps he, the boy, was really an outsider. Now as a father he may feel that same sense of being pushed out, of being physically jolted into an awareness of the threesome and the loss of his partner's primary attention. Under such conditions, and because socialization to the masculine role discourages him from articulating to himself or his partner how this new situation is affecting him emotionally, he may find a temporary replacement for his partner by taking a lover.

When Laura pressed Pete about what was happening

between them sexually, he found himself pleased by her attention and pursuit of him. He told her how much he missed her. He didn't mention the affair but dropped his lover and gravitated back to Laura. Laura felt uneasy and guilty for having neglected Pete and they both put a lot of energy into their relationship again. Several months after they had resumed sleeping together regularly again, they left their child with the grandparents and went away together. Pete, in a particularly close moment, enjoying having Laura all to himself again, confessed his affair. He had felt terribly guilty all of a sudden and before he knew what was happening he had told Laura about it. Although she appeared quite understanding, she immediately sank inside. She felt lousy and betrayed. From that time on, she felt less and less eager to make love. Each time they were physically intimate, she would find herself being reminded of his affair and would get upset. She tried to hide this from Pete with the result that she felt increasingly mistrustful and angry towards him. She avoided initiating sex and, without even being aware of it, put her energy into other things.

Between the two of them, the following dynamics were at work. Pete had felt abandoned by Laura; at the same time, he had himself abandoned her by removing himself from her and the baby. Out of anger and a difficulty with containing his own dependency needs in the short term, he started up with an eager student. When Laura showed her availability once again, he transferred his dependency needs back to her and their relationship. His fear of intimacy surfaced when they were reunited. As a protection against the closeness, guilt about his affair surfaced and not knowing how to handle it he unconsciously used it as a wedge in their relationship. To Laura, he transmitted a threat. She heard the news of his affair as a warning not to turn her attention away from him for a moment. At a deeper level, his 'confession' played on her own feelings of insecurity. She felt she'd been wrong to trust Pete, she had allowed herself to be lulled into a false sense of security. She felt very hurt indeed. The other woman, and now all Pete's female students, seemed very threatening to her. Her own fear of intimacy joined with Pete's and the affair became the reason why they weren't able to be as close as they had been. It was Pete's inability to cope with his dependency needs and his fear and anger (the feelings which were behind the guilt) at being, as he experienced it, abandoned by Laura, that had stirred up both of their fears of intimacy and close relating. They came to live with the distance. Laura was always worried that Pete would take up with someone else and that became the reason she couldn't get close. Pete was annoyed that she was withdrawn. He felt he had been honest and that showed how committed he was to her and now he was being punished. He resented her distance and was impatient with her. He wanted more sexual love and contact. In our practice we have seen how a man may have an affair as a response to the complex changes he is experiencing in relation to his partner's pregnancy, his dependency needs, her dependency needs and his unconscious fantasies of the baby's dependency.

Jack and Irene have been married for four years. In Irene's seventh month of pregnancy Jack had an affair. It was the first sexual affair he had had since his marriage. Just before the baby was born Jack told Irene about the affair and that he had stopped it. During the first year of the baby's life Jack went through an emotional upheaval. Irene couldn't depend on him for assistance for herself or the baby because Jack was always too distressed about something in his life — work, the car, illness, one crisis after another. Irene felt frightened by Jack's behaviour and finally insisted he see a psychotherapist.

Vincent had his first extra-marital affair when Adrianne was pregnant. He didn't know why he sought out the encounter and felt quite uninterested in the 'other' woman. He slept with Jean twice. Like a dream that comes and goes he forgot all about it. The next time he had an affair was when Adrianne was six months pregnant with their second

child. Again the affair was not a serious departure or event in
his life. Only the day after he slept with Rosalie did he
remember that Adrianne had been pregnant the first time
too. He wondered about this.

Men seeking sexual contact with another woman when
their wives are pregnant is not as uncommon as one might
wish to believe. The most common explanation of this
behaviour is that the wife's body is too big, she can't have sex
and the man, for whom sex is like appetite — a natural drive,
instinct — must seek relief somewhere .... Having a clearer
understanding of men's dependency needs offers a different
understanding of this phenomenon.

On a conscious level Irene's pregnancy thrilled Jack. He
wanted to have children and he was tremendously excited
about the anticipated arrival of their first child. The level of
distress which Jack experienced after the birth and his
subsequent therapy experience enabled him not only to
understand the 'breakdown' but also to understand why he
sought a sexual affair during Irene's pregnancy. Jack unconsciously felt threatened by the arrival of his child.
Suddenly he felt an interference in his attachment with
Irene. Irene talked more and more about the baby as the
pregnancy progressed and when Irene excitedly reported
the baby's movements inside her (especially as they lay in
bed at night) Jack felt twinges of jealousy. She was involved
with someone else in that bed — it was no longer just the two
of them. The jealous feelings were too unsettling and Jack
pushed them away. He tried, instead, to continue to show his
excitement and delight and to share in those moments with
Irene. He had an affair. He unconsciously tried to make
himself feel secure by being with a woman who was wholly
available. He needed to be alone with a woman — the
tension of the triangle was too upsetting. He needed
reassurance. Irene's pregnancy rekindled unconscious infantile memories Jack had of the interrupted twosome he
had with his own mother and the triangle he lived in with his
father and mother. Jack was an only child and so the triangle
was never broken — he either was alone or in the triangle. In

the first years of their marriage Jack was the happiest he had
ever been in his life. He finally had someone special for
himself and someone to whom he was special. The birth of
their child was psychologically jolting for Jack because his
dependency needs were being threatened once again — his
woman was going to have another strong attachment. He
felt this as a loss; he felt alone and frightened. The affair was
an attempt to get someone for himself, to get reassurance.
Just like dad had mother, mother had dad, now Irene had
the baby and who did Jack have? His breakdown in the first
year of the baby's life was Jack's regression. His continual
crisis was his statement that things were not all right; that he
couldn't take care of himself; that he needed to get the
attention and the care that the baby was getting. Jack's
dependency needs were exposed.

Vincent's affairs had a different meaning. There were
traces of jealousy in Vincent's feeling that the baby was
getting what he had been getting — that is, that unconsciously Vincent feared that Adrianne's love and attention would *all* go to the baby and he would lose her. But the
more predominant feeling for Vincent was that he felt
trapped. Some of these feelings were conscious — he worried about the financial responsibilities of having a child; he
was aware of feeling that having a child really meant that he
was an adult and forced him to feel adult commitment.
Unconsciously several things were bubbling away beneath
the surface. First was the effect of Adrianne's increased
dependency on him. Adrianne herself admitted that during
her pregnancies she was the most aware of her own
dependency feelings. She needed Vincent to be very
attentive to her emotionally; she needed to feel his being
there and holding her as she 'held' the foetus inside her.
(When she isn't pregnant Adrianne fights these feelings in
herself and doesn't show them to Vincent.) So Vincent had
to give more emotionally than he was used to and unconsciously he felt depleted and somewhat resentful. After
all, his own child-rearing did not equip him for all this
emotional caretaking so he felt he was giving something

above and beyond what was called for. One aspect of his
sexual affair was an attempt to re-establish the balance. He
wanted to be with a woman who did not demand too much
from him emotionally and through whom he could revive
his depleted resources by having her be attentive, giving,
interested, in awe, etc. of him. The second unconscious
motivation and perhaps the more significant one was that
Vincent needed to affirm his separateness. Some of the
boundaries of merger with Adrianne were getting too
blurred. The unborn infant represented their merger.
Vincent's feelings of responsibility and commitment were
attached to the unconscious feelings of involvement. He felt
trapped. He needed to break free of this unconscious murky
attachment to a woman — he needed to experience himself
in the 'old' ways, as an individual. He, like Jack, needed a
woman to be available to him. Someone to whom he
didn't have to give much and whom he could 'use' to get a
stronger sense of himself.

The gestation and birth of a child, then, evokes emotions
in men which very often are to do with their dependency on
women. A pregnant wife makes visible the ultimate dependency which the man, himself, once had on a woman.
There are reminders of his own infantile dependency needs,
of his own attachment to his mother, at the same time as a
reminder of the triangle — of the mother-father-child nexus
— the triangle which has already once in his life caused him
emotional upset and readjustment.

When Rosemary was pregnant Neil withdrew from sex
altogether. Rosemary was terribly upset about this as she felt
particularly vulnerable and wanted to feel physically close.
She imagined that he was turned off because her body was
unattractive, distended and swollen. When she talked to
Neil, complicated factors emerged about his relationship to
the pregnancy. It made Rosemary seem awfully strong and
independent in his eyes. She had this almost magical power
to nourish a baby inside her, to create new life. He felt
jealous of this capacity and somewhat in awe of it. Rosemary

now had something that he knew he could never have and he felt wretched. In addition, up to that point in the relationship, he had always seen himself as the secure and loved one, and Rosemary's attention had been so distinctly focused on him that he felt important and wanted. Now not only did he feel somewhat in awe of Rosemary, but he felt a bit rejected. Her good feelings about being pregnant diverted some of the attention away from him. He was left without the constant booster he was used to, and his own negative feelings about himself seeped through. He held out sexually for two reasons. First, he now wanted Rosemary to come after him, to make him feel that he was wanted — even if he then rejected her. Second, he felt that he would damage the baby with his penis. He knew rationally that this was ridiculous, and he wouldn't have agreed to couple therapy if he hadn't been so utterly overwhelmed by these destructive feelings.

Neil's experience hit a nerve that many men have peeked at but had a hard time facing. In with this dreadful fear of hurting the baby were Neil's negative and angry feelings about being pushed out by the pregnancy. Unconsciously he may have *wanted* to hurt the baby. Although Neil was unable to acknowledge his dependency on Rosemary, it was very strong indeed. His distance was proportional to the amount of need he did have of her. He couldn't bear to think of himself as being dependent on anyone. The very idea seemed to threaten his sense of masculinity and so he retreated from that reality into its very opposite until his needy feelings caught up with him in this scary, destructive form. During the couple therapy Neil came to face his negative feelings towards the baby as such, as well as the baby-type feelings of dependency that he had been trying to get away from in himself.

The entry of children into a relationship, then, centrally touches the chord of emotional dependency. As we have seen in earlier chapters, the achievement of intimate relationships is an intricate process. The potential of an intimate relationship arrives with the birth of every child. Two people developing a loving, caring relationship to their offspring and opening up themselves and their own intimate relationship to this new person is another link in the chain of human emotional experience.

7

Friendship Between Women

From what we have seen of emotional dependency needs and women's and men's relation to nurturance, it becomes apparent that women's relationships with one another must play important and sustaining parts in their lives. Because of women's social conditioning, and because the mother-daughter relationship sets the blueprint for so much of what is to come in adult relationships, relationships between women are complex. Strikingly little attention has been paid to women's friendships. One doesn't find much written about it explicitly in magazines or novels. One can count on one hand the number of films which have been made in which the focus is a relationship between women. There are television shows in which two women are the central characters but the emphasis is always on the ways in which other people come and go in their lives, the crazy situations they get into with men or work. What goes on between them or what they get from each other is in the background of the plot. Most remarkable, to us, is the absence in psychology textbooks and teaching of any discussion of the role that women play in each other's emotional lives. Extensive theoretical debate about the effect of mothers in everyone's lives is just beginning. There are texts about adolescence and the importance of peer groups; of triangles in children's friendships; of the critical nature of acceptance and rejection in childhood and adolescent friendships. But nowhere in the literature (except perhaps very recently from feminist writings) is there discussion and observation about the centrality of women's friendships and relationships with sisters, aunts, grandmothers, etc., in their emotional and psychological lives.[1]

It therefore seems essential to put into black and white the blindingly obvious fact that women have always relied on and depended on each other emotionally. Perhaps in our society today some of the support is less obvious than it was years ago and still is today in other cultures where women gather together and rely on each other for child care, getting provisions for the family, doing laundry, etc. The remnants of this are most evident in immigrant family groups and working-class families where mothers and sisters are extremely important to one another and where there is daily contact and involvement in the extended family life. Over the years women have become more isolated in the home, and this may be especially true for working- and middle-class women, where the washing machine, for example, is in the home and where large supermarkets take the place of smaller neighbourhood markets and shops. Yet, even within the isolation of so many women's day-to-day lives, they find ways of spending time with one another and forming friendships. In work situations, whether it be on the shop floor, in coffee-break time, the lunch break, the office hall, women talk to one another about their joys and woes and their daily 'mundane' experiences. It may be at the PTA or the playground, the laundrette, the bridge game, the community-neighbourhood association, the renowned coffee morning — women tell girlfriends about the problems they are having with their kids or their husbands or their mothers or their in-laws or their bosses and supervisors. Women seem to know that there is a receptive ear ready to listen and commiserate, a listening ear ready to identify with their anger, disappointments, pride and pleasure.

Joanne and Linda are next-door neighbours. They became friends when Linda and Alan moved into their semi-detached house after they were married. Joanne had lived in

1. Helen Deutsch does recognize their importance but warns us of the dangers that can flow from close female friendships in adolescence.

the same street for several years with her husband Mike. When Linda was moving into the house Joanne went over to introduce herself and to offer cups of coffee and a sandwich. Over the next few years they developed a friendship. They became pregnant round about the same time and after they gave up their jobs, they began to spend more and more time together discussing how their pregnancies were going, how each of them was planning for the arrival of the baby, and so on. Their relationship was supportive and filled spaces in each of their lives. Their daily contact and encouragement with the growing babies provided essential support. Mike and Alan were unaware of how much their wives depended on and were nourished by each other.

Women's friendships are a curious social phenomenon. On the one hand they are completely obvious and assumed and yet they are also invisible to a large extent. So much attention is focused on heterosexual coupling, marriage, dating, that the fact of women's relationships with one another goes largely unnoticed. We might say that the relationships themselves take on a second-class status reflecting women's second-class position in society. We are largely unconscious of the way in which the lack of recognition of these friendships relegates them to a position of lesser importance to our emotional well-being than relationships with men.

Our mothers' women friends were as important to them as ours are to us. The difference is that we have begun to recognize the importance of these relationships and to value them. Our mothers talked with their friends about problems in their marriages, difficulties with their children, pleasure in the achievements of their children, worries about the finances, the cost of living, etc. But the time spent with a woman friend did not carry the weight of social approval and significance that being with a man did. It was spare-time activity, daily 'time-passing' activity while the men were at work or out together at football or in the living room watching sport together on TV or out playing poker or bowling. Time with women friends was seen as something

arranged around the schedule of your husband and the times
he made it clear he would not be available to be with you.
The actual importance of the women in each other's lives
was no less than it is now but the perception of the
relationships was different — it was *seen* as less important.
We can now look at these 'time-passing' activities as the
refuelling period, the nourishment, the discharge of tensions
and anger; a communication process that recharged the
battery for our mothers to go back into the home and
continue to give out to children and husbands.

Ruth, Marion, Eleanor and Jean are all women in their early
sixties. They have known one another and been friends for
nearly thirty years. Their friendships began when their
children were young and at school and the women got
together through their children's involvement with one
another. Over the years their friendships took many forms,
ranging from great closeness to some distance, and with
various 'couples' being closer to one another than others, etc.
They shared with each other their feelings during times of
joy such as marriages of the children and the births of grand-
children, as well as at times of personal crises and sorrow.
When Eleanor's husband died the others were all very
involved in caring for her. Throughout the years, whether it
was out at lunch, at one another's house over a cup of
coffee or during one of their numerous phone conversations,
they shared details of their daily lives, and so were all up
to date on each other's emotional state. They shared with
each other in ways which were very different from how
they shared with their husbands and families. With one
another they felt a sense of equality, of camaraderie, that
comes from having a common experience. They didn't feel
responsible for one another in the way they felt responsible
for their husbands or children. They received from and gave
to one another a tremendous amount, and their friendships
were and continue to be critical parts of the fabric of each of
their lives.

The women's liberation movement in the last few years

has legitimated women's friendships. It is only in recent years that women have been able to recognize that their relationships with other women are terribly important to them; that they are as important as their relationships with men. It is only in recent years that women have begun to see and talk about what it is they get from other women and what they get from men — to see the differences in these relationships and see that each is important in its own way. It is only in recent years that women have been able to spend time with their women friends and feel that it is just what they want to be doing and exactly where they want to be — and not an activity that is second best. It is a new experience and somewhat of a struggle for women to arrange dates with women friends as a priority and without planning them around the schedule of their men. Women have always depended on one another for certain kinds of personal exchange and communication. In our society women's communications are often devalued and seen as chatter while men's conversations are seen to be of great relevance. Men talk of politics and ideas whilst women are seen to talk only about clothes, recipes and housework. The imbalance between women's and men's experiences is talked about in terms of what women lack. Rarely is it suggested that the limitations that men have in talking about personal matters is equally a problem, or that women's ability to talk about their own lives is a strength and a social virtue. The undermining of women's communications is part and parcel of the overall social undermining of women's friendships.

This new view of women's friendships, then, lets us see how much women actually give to one another; how they depend on each other for emotional support and for a receptive ear; how their shared experience with children and husbands and their identifications with one another make for rich human contact and interaction. We can see how sisters and mothers can be leaned on and demands and favours requested of them that women would never bring to their men. But women's relationships are not all rosy and nurturing. They are multi-faceted and complex. Women are often disappointed by their friends; they may feel anger towards them which often is very difficult to express; they may feel competitive and envious.

Freud's concept of transference in psychoanalytic theory (see pages 98-103) has much to offer us in our understanding of women's friendships. Transference takes place in practically all relationships to some extent and this is certainly no less true in the arena of friendships between women. In fact it is perhaps within these relationships that women bring most of their transference potential into play. For there are so many parallels and nuances between that first, familiar relationship with a woman — one's mother — and the later relationships a woman forms with others of her own gender. All of the issues we have described in earlier chapters that make up women's psychology — issues of merger, boundaries, expectations, disappointments, betrayal, abandonment, loss, autonomy, are threads in the fabric of female friendships.

Emotional dependency needs are a part of women's friendships and may look quite different from dependency needs in a sexual relationship. Often people do not have one friend but several and there are different degrees of intimacy in different friendships. Different things may be needed from each different friend, and different friends share different interests. So, for example, Ann and Lea always went to art galleries and photography exhibitions together because they shared this interest. They had detailed and vital discussions about the art world and new work that was coming out and how that compared to other work, etc. They never talked about their emotional lives and how they *felt* in their workplaces or in their other relationships. In that way they were actually quite shy with one another. Lea had one close friend, Mary, with whom she uncovered her deepest personal feelings, disappointments and vulnerability.

Whereas in some ways we are 'prepared' for the range of intense feelings of disappointment, jealousy, anger and love in intimate sexual relationships, we are less aware of the inevitability of these same emotions popping up in friend-ships. We may expect and tolerate our 'irrational' behaviour and responses to a lover or husband and yet be surprised and uncomfortable about having these feelings towards a friend. They may seem out of place, wrong and awkward.

Naomi and Carol shared a flat. They were good friends. They spent many evenings at home together, cooking, telling each other about their work activities, their love affairs, etc. Naomi was an editor at a publishing house and Carol was an actress. Carol's work was erratic. From time to time she had parts in fringe theatre repertory companies and the like, but much of the time she was unemployed and going to acting and dancing classes. They each dated various men, although Naomi mostly dated Josh, a man with whom she had lived several years before. Each had different friends who were in their respective work worlds and several old friends from college days. Sometimes Naomi or Carol spent time with the other's friends when they came to the flat or occasionally they invited the other out if they were meeting a friend and the other had nothing to do that particular evening. They had some minor fights to do with housework standards, the way phone messages were taken and once about the way Carol felt Naomi always finished the 'special' food in the house without thinking of her and what she was going to eat for dinner. But mostly they got along with one another and were supportive in their friendship.

Things changed in their relationship after a series of events. Carol was offered a part in a play. The play was successful and the actors decided to form a theatre group in order to continue to perform together. Carol became more and more involved in the group. She spent several evenings a week at meetings and rehearsals. She became friendly with Jeannine, another woman in the group. When she was at home she told Naomi all about the new developments, the ins and outs of the meetings, the personalities, etc. At first Naomi listened with great interest and she offered

suggestions and 'gossiped' about the people with great
enthusiasm. Then Naomi started to feel angry with Carol.
During the evenings when Carol was out Naomi noticed the
housework Carol didn't do. She was annoyed that Carol was
hardly eating at home anymore, hardly shopping or cooking.
Naomi began to go into her bedroom at night before Carol
got home because she felt she didn't want to hear all about
the theatre group. She was upset and angry and she didn't
want to show this to Carol. Naomi often left for work in the
morning before Carol was up so they started to see each
other less and less frequently. When they were together at
home for the evening or part of the evening, it felt tense.
Naomi started to stay over at Josh's more. She complained to
Josh about Carol and how she was so involved in her 'thing'
that it was getting impossible to live with her. Naomi was
irritated and miserable. Carol was feeling angry, guilty and
confused. She felt that Naomi was passively aggressive, that
she had changed and that things were not right but she didn't
know why. She felt angry with Naomi for acting so 'bitchy'
towards her and for always complaining about the housework or about what Carol wasn't doing right. Carol felt like
she was living with her mother again. She avoided Naomi as
much as possible. Outside the flat, when she was with other
friends or with her theatre group, she felt fine — why did she
have to feel so lousy when she came home?

Few women friends are able to confront one another or
talk easily to one another about upsetting feelings in the
friendship. It takes time to bring up the feelings and to talk
directly to a friend about them, and many times women find
it extremely difficult to express anger to a friend. The
difficulties women have in expressing anger, and the
feelings of shame that can be associated with angry or
critical feelings towards a friend, often prevent women
from tackling problems in their relationships. This was the
case with Naomi and Carol. But let's take a close look and
dissect what exactly was happening between them.

Naomi and Carol had become emotionally dependent on
one another and yet this dependency was never openly

acknowledged. Because they shared a flat and saw a lot of one another easily, they never had to make their wish to spend time together explicit by arranging dates. Naomi was more conscious of her dependency on Josh and wouldn't have thought that Carol's activities could have affected her so. When Carol got the part in the play and became involved with the theatre group, Naomi felt abandoned and excluded. She felt competitive feelings towards Carol's new friend Jeannine. She imagined that Carol and Jeannine had lots of excitement about their new relationship and that they had outrageous and way-out times together. Naomi felt boring and dull by comparison. Part of the negativity that she transmitted to Carol was in fact a projection of some of the feelings that she was having about herself. She felt unattractive and negative. She felt left behind and bereft. These feelings came across as anger and unspoken criticism of the people Carol was now involved with. Naomi wasn't conscious of all her feelings and so she could not sit down and tell Carol about them. They were a confused mass inside her and they came out in all kinds of distorted and distressing ways. Naomi was deeply upset and ashamed about her feelings of jealousy and competitiveness towards Jeannine. She was more 'prepared' for these kinds of feelings in relation to Josh and other women, but having this reaction to a girlfriend confused and upset her even more.

On the other side of this dynamic Carol had her own set of unconscious expectations and reactions to Naomi's upset. Carol experienced Naomi's passive anger as a hold on her. She felt constrained and undermined. She wished that Naomi could have been supportive and encouraging of her new connections with the theatre group. She herself was surprised to find that she felt guilty about her activities apart from Naomi and unconsciously felt that she was betraying and abandoning her. She was upset and angry about the unspoken messages she thought she was getting not to be independent and autonomous. She was experiencing (unconsciously) transference feelings towards Naomi that were really about dynamics in her relationship with her mother. Carol felt more and more that she wanted to be away from the apartment. When she was away she felt free; when she was at home she felt constricted and depressed. She didn't want to feel Naomi's needs for her; she did not want to be aware of Naomi's dependency because it felt like her mother's dependency. She wanted to blot it all out for fear that she would get trapped by Naomi's needs. She felt guilty and angry. She was acting towards Naomi in the same way that she had acted towards her mother — that is, she ignored the need and tried to push it away. In fact, Carol's mother did have a strong attachment to and need for her daughter. She was a housewife and mother who never was able to develop herself and her own potential. She lived through her children. She loved to hear about Carol's activities because they filled a gap in her life. Carol's mother had an unconscious need to hold on to Carol and not allow her to separate and be autonomous in the world. It was too frightening a proposition for her mother to be left on her own. And so Carol's reaction to Naomi's feelings of abandonment, envy, attachment, was in many ways blown out of proportion to the real situation between them. Carol couldn't look at the actual situation without bringing with her all her unconscious attachments with her mother. She unconsciously felt that her autonomy and selfhood could exist only by fighting off and radically detaching herself from the woman she loved and was close to. She couldn't afford to feel her own dependency because these needs endangered her sense of self and well-being. She could not imagine maintaining the attachment, experiencing the interdependency and still being able to be separate.

Monika and Jane had been good friends for four years. They were both physiotherapists and met in graduate school during their training. They each lived with men but saw the relationship between them as equally important as — even though different from — their sexual relationships. They spoke to each other daily, saw each other three or four times a week and were very involved in each other's lives. They brought their men together, introduced other friends to each other, talked about politics together and shopped together. Monika and Jane decided that working in hospitals was very draining and depressing and that they could rarely follow their work through with one patient, which they saw as terribly important to the treatment. They discussed their work extensively and finally reached the conclusion that they should open a health spa that also offered physio-therapy services. This was a big financial plunge for them but they took the risk. They took out bank loans, got accountants and lawyers, bought health equipment and machinery — all jointly. For the first six months, although there was a lot of pressure and tension, things went smoothly. They managed to discuss all the issues, share the worries, the annoyances, etc. Then things started to change. Gradually Monika noticed that she was feeling annoyed by Jane. She didn't like the way Jane handled people on the telephone; she felt that Jane was very tense and bossy. Similarly, Jane was angry with Monika. She felt that Monika wasn't moving fast enough and that she was not wise enough in business matters. The tension began to build under the surface because neither of them directly confronted the other with her feelings. Each day was worse for both of them. All the things that were bothering them became more and more dominant so that they were unable to enjoy and appreciate other aspects of the friendship. They began to bicker openly and the tension at the health spa was so great that it was a very stressful place for each of them to be. They didn't call one another in the evenings as they had always done in the past; they didn't go out for lunch or for a chatty drink; they didn't tell one another about their loves and fights with their boyfriends. They came into work — did the work under great tension — and went home.

After several weeks of this excruciating tension between them, the summer vacation drew closer. They decided to close the spa for one month and agreed that they each needed the time away from work and each other. In the time

they were apart several things happened which were to be
the keys to the solution to their difficulties. First of all
through the physical separation from each other and the spa
they each realized that they had been feeling swamped.
They had had to fight to maintain their own sense of self
within what often seemed like an enclosed, merged system.
Being apart allowed them to feel their own separate
identities and, thus, to work out what appeared to be going
wrong between them. They began to miss each other. Jane
was able to think about Monika — at a distance — and
therefore as her own separate self, and these thoughts
allowed for some positive feelings to re-emerge. Similarly
Monika felt herself missing Jane, and the criticisms she had
felt previously seemed to recede into the background.

When they came back from their holidays Monika called
Jane and each acknowledged that it was good to hear the
other's voice and that they should get together 'socially'
before starting back at the spa. They discussed their
commitments to one another, their missing one another.
They cried and laughed and then had the big fight in which
they each 'got out' all of the pent-up grievances they had
accumulated over the previous six months. Some of the
grievances were disputed, but by and large each let the other
be heard and there was some appreciation for and acceptance of angry feelings. Their own summary of the events
was that they had become too merged because of their joint
responsibility for the spa. There was a pattern in the
grievances: assumptions were being made by each about
the other that had nothing to do with establishing what the
other actually felt or intended to do about a given situation.
That is, each acted towards the other as if she were an
extension of herself. Their fighting and irritation was an
attempt to separate from the merger. They found that the
same problem did not repeat itself and that they treated
each other with more awareness and recognition of separate
identity after that time.

This needed commitment from both of them. They each
took responsibility for being more aware of how they were

relating to the other. They each had to face painful things in themselves about how much they wanted things their own way, and they came to see that, just as in their relationships with men where they had to compromise and adjust to one another, so too with their close woman friend did each have to take account of the wishes of the other and make compromises when they felt differently about something.

Jane and Monika were able to save their friendship and build on it because they could sit face to face and declare their grievances and their feelings for each other. Their being apart for a brief period enabled them to miss the other and thereby feel the importance of each other in their lives. Criticism and the declaration of angry and hurt feelings is an effort that people must make in the struggle to have good relationships. In couples there is an assumption that fights and struggles must go on, that they are a part of what intimate relationships are and that, as unpleasant as they often can be, they must occur because it's only 'natural' that people experience a full range of feelings in relationships — loving and critical, angry, disappointed, etc. What Jane and Monika were able to do was not only have the direct discussion but, perhaps more importantly, to validate the importance of the relationship. They knew that this friendship was a central part of each of their lives, and therefore as uncomfortable as it may have been they forced themselves to confront the situation. They stated their need for one another and acknowledged that the loss of the friendship would be a great tragedy for each of them.

Jane and Monika's experience of assuming the other was just like her can be seen in different forms in friendships. Because women are so attuned to others and because women feel less defined in themselves, more unsure of themselves, the distinctions between friends may become blurred. For example, a woman may act towards her friend in the same way as she herself would like to be treated if she were in her friend's situation, when this may not reflect what the friend actually wants or needs. Joan was very distraught when her mother died. When she was with her friend Marie,

she was keenly aware of the way in which Marie avoided
any discussion about the death. Marie, on the other hand,
was also aware of not talking about the death of Joan's
mother because she felt that this would be upsetting for her.
In fact, it was the level of upset which the death evoked in
Marie that kept her from seeing the actual need of her friend
to talk about the death and from responding appropriately
to that need. When her grandmother had died in Ireland
when she was a girl, Marie had felt extremely embarrassed,
upset and humiliated when anyone talked aloud about the
death to her. When Joan's mother died Marie was operating
out of unconscious behaviour. She was acting towards Joan
in the way she 'wished' everyone would have acted towards
her at the time of her grandmother's death. She felt that she
was acting in Joan's interest when in fact her own unconscious need got in the way of her seeing Joan's need.

Another example of women friends acting unconsciously
towards one another is the friend who can be supportive in
crisis but who is unable positively to nurture her friend
towards fulfilment or autonomy. Society's desire to keep
women in their place and the feeling that women's success in
the world is threatening finds its way insidiously even into
friendships between women. Randy was the best friend in
the world when her friends were in crisis. Any kind of upset
or outrage would be met by Randy with support and com-
miseration for the 'victim'. It's no surprise that Randy
became a lawyer because she unconsciously identified with
a victim of injustice and she had strong needs and impulses
to fight back. Randy's friend Susan spoke of this in therapy
and began to notice a pattern in their relating: every time
Susan was upset Randy was emotionally supportive to her,
but when Susan was happy and feeling successful either in
her love life or her work Randy hardly responded to that at
all. When they talked, Randy would merely acknowledge
Susan's descriptions of what she felt to be important
achievements by saying, 'Uhmm, that's great.' But there was
no fuel, no energy, no real enthusiasm or engagement for
these experiences. Susan began to see that Randy's vitality

and energy (of which there was plenty) were only stimulated when something upsetting happened to Susan or when Susan registered some sort of complaint about her situation. Again, in a similar fashion to Marie, Randy's unconscious was in operation with her women friends in a way that prevented her from actually seeing their real needs. She could only relate energetically when she could unconsciously identify with the experience of her friend. In fact, Randy found it very difficult to fight for herself and transferred all of her own feelings of being a victim, of anger, of acute sensitivity to injustices, of having to put right what was wrong, etc., on to her relationships with others and then fought on their behalf. Being happy with what she had achieved was impossible for Randy because unconsciously she felt that recognition of her own virtues would negate her legitimate anger about the 'injustices' she had experienced. She couldn't let go of the defence because she felt too fragile and vulnerable. It wasn't until Susan began to point some of this out to her and to describe the ways in which she felt that Randy related to her that Randy became at all aware of these unconscious issues. By transferring her own psychology on to her friends and having one of them feed back what it felt like, Randy could begin to examine how this affected her own life.

As long as women's friendships don't become sexual or pushed to the forefront, society allows them. It is in women's friendships that we can see other examples of the damage and deprivation that women suffer. Even between the best of friends comparisons are made about what each has in her life, and from the unconscious feelings of deprivation and the belief that one may never get what one wants and needs, women consciously feel competitive and envious towards one another. Painfully we see the ways in which women friends unconsciously attempt to hold each other down — to stay merged together in the deprivation they feel. Achievements, successes, recognitions, new boyfriends, can make friends feel left behind, abandoned. Women hate having to face those feelings and are ashamed of them. It's very difficult to understand why they arise. And yet, when we analyse women's relationships with one another with an understanding of women's oppression and of the mother-daughter relationship, we see that these feelings are inevitable in modern society. As long as women do not feel good in themselves, whole within themselves, and substantive, and as long as they are encouraged to look to other people (especially men) to establish their place in the world, then they will be frightened of other women's successes. They will feel less worthy by comparison; they will feel abandoned and left behind; they will feel what is missing in their own lives. If women succeed in holding each other back, then these feelings are somewhat alleviated — they can remain hidden.

Alicia and Sue are both single women in their late twenties. They share an apartment and are good friends. Lots of their time together is spent talking about why they don't meet men, why there are no men around, how they are wanting to meet men, etc. Alicia suddenly found herself interested in two men in her post-graduate class. She talked with one of them on one day and the next day she flirted with the other. That night she told Sue all about it. They both laughed and giggled about the possible 'moves' that Alicia could now make. The next day when they got home Sue told Alicia that a friend of hers at work had invited her for dinner the following Saturday night and that she had invited a friend of her husband's for Sue to meet. Immediately upon hearing this Alicia felt depressed. She felt empty, blue and just miserable. In discussing these feelings in therapy Alicia felt terribly ashamed. She loved Sue a lot and wanted her to be happy. She wanted Sue to meet a man, so why should she have these awful feelings of competition? It seemed that Sue's having a concrete date made Alicia feel that her two flirtations were just nonsense, that nothing real existed. She wasn't able to hold on to her own excitement and anticipation about what she might have to look forward to and felt that she would *never* get what she was wanting.

Given Alicia's psychology and her unconscious certainty about being inevitably disappointed, it was too difficult for her to believe that she might get something she wanted. It would have been difficult for her to remain excited about the flirtations for very long anyway and Sue's date — that is, Alicia's fantasy that Sue was actually getting what she herself would not get — brought her despair immediately to the surface. Envy is very common between women. It is part and parcel of the experience of emotional deprivation. One easily and readily imagines that another person is getting so much more than oneself. In many cases this may be true. (Women who have had brothers often tell of their envy that their brothers were given to in ways that *they* weren't.)

Differences in the lives of women friends can, therefore, be problematic. Many women find it possible to have close friends whose lives are strikingly similar to their own — whether professionally or domestically. For instance, dependency needs may be unevenly balanced in a friendship where one woman has an intimate, sexual relationship and the other doesn't. The woman who is on her own may have a greater need for contact and emotional exchange than the woman in a 'marriage' who may be getting some of her needs satisfied by her partner. The tangle of expectation and disappointment is painful to live with, as is the guilt which may be felt by the friend.

A woman's jealousy about her friend's 'having a man' when she didn't used to be understood (and still is to a large extent) as purely competitive. The emphasis was on the man as the important factor — the prize, so to speak. In fact, that particular triangle is much more complex and much richer. It may be that a woman envies her friend for being in a relationship with a particular man whom she likes very much. It may be that the friend envies her friend for being involved with a man at all — any man, despite who he is. Seeing these feelings only in that light, however, leaves out the woman's sense of abandonment and loss because the socially valid attachment, the attachment that is recognized as existing, is the tie between the man and the woman and *not* the tie between the two women. Involvement with a man threatens women's friendships because it undermines them. People are seen as either alone — unattached — or in a heterosexual couple. These kinds of social expectations contribute to people's distress, loneliness and feelings of isolation and being unloved. If one is not in a couple then one feels undesirable, unlovable. A woman or a man can have two or three very close friends who love her or him dearly but that will not alleviate the feelings of aloneness in a society that undervalues friendships and puts the spotlight on heterosexual couple arrangements as the only *real* loving relationships between people.

Women's 'competition' for a man replays the developmental imperative for all girls — that is, that the original loving attachment to her mother must be broken and the girl must turn her attention to her father and win his love. She learns that he is powerful and important and that one day she too, like mother, must have a man of her own. The girl's original experience of being in a 'couple' with her mother is threatened when she becomes aware of her parents' involvement and the important place her father has in her mother's life. For an adult woman, a friend's fighting with her or competing with her for a man both negates and denies the connection between the women (which is probably what hurts most) and recreates the possibility of a triangle in which one person is excluded from the special intimacy that the other two share.

Sometimes men are jealous of women's friendships. This may be because they envy the intimacy between the women and wish that they could have similar relationships with men friends, or it may be that a man feels threatened by the attachment his woman has to another person and the ease women seem to have communicating about their personal lives. He may be subconsciously aware of the things the woman friend gives to his partner that he doesn't give, or he may resent the intimate nature of the confidence his woman shares with her friends — about things which he may believe should remain private affairs between him and his woman.

His own dependency within the relationship and his unconscious insecurity are revealed in his attitude towards the friendships his woman has with other women.

When Michael first became involved with Arlene he knew that Beth was not only Arlene's flatmate but Arlene's dearest friend. Arlene had introduced Michael to Beth by their third date and often mentioned Beth when telling Michael a story about herself. Michael didn't think too much about this because it was all familiar — other women he had dated in the past had girlfriends whom they talked about and did things with. In fact, he knew that being introduced to a close girlfriend was a good sign — it meant that the woman liked him and wanted to show him to her friend. He even felt aware of somehow having to get the approval of the girlfriend in order for things to proceed smoothly. So at first Michael was very charming and friendly to Beth. He told her jokes and stories and directed a lot of attention towards her, giving her signs of inclusion when the three of them were together. He needed Beth's acceptance. A few months later in their relationship, Arlene told Michael that there had been a period of time in which she was involved with women sexually. She felt that, although overall it had been a good experience for her, she had come to feel that she was still primarily interested in men sexually. Michael felt a bit shocked and disturbed by this new information but felt that, as a man living in 'the eighties', this was something that he should be able to handle. Michael asked Arlene several questions, one of which was whether Beth was a lover. Arlene told Michael that she wasn't and had never been. But something changed for Michael from that time onwards. He watched the interaction between Beth and Arlene now through different spectacles. Their closeness began to irritate him. He felt angry with Arlene when she would phone Beth to say she wouldn't be home for the night. He was furious when Beth called Arlene at his apartment. He felt his private space was being invaded and that Beth had access to Arlene at any time. He began to say little things —

point out different aspects of Beth's personality in a critical
way. He told Arlene that he thought Beth was too attached
and possessive of Arlene, and that Beth was hostile to him.
Arlene felt very uncomfortable about her lover being critical
of her best friend; Beth began to like Michael less and less
because she felt he was not very nice to her and seemed to
disagree with everything she said; and Michael interpreted
Beth's cold shoulder towards him as a sign that she was
competing with him and that she wanted to get rid of him.
Beth and Arlene began to see less of each other.

Michael's difficult feelings about Arlene and Beth's
relationship only came to the fore when he became aware of
the level of attachment that Arlene was able to attain with
women. His knowledge of Arlene's lesbian relationships
disturbed Michael on a very deep level. He felt shaken,
threatened and angry. His changing attitude to Beth was
happening more or less on an unconscious level — that is,
Michael was not fully aware of his feelings about Arlene's
involvement with another woman or his feelings about
lesbianism. Consciously he was only aware of feeling critical
of Beth and annoyed by her behaviour. He was somewhat
aware of his possessiveness and his jealousy of the friendship. He wanted to distance Beth and Arlene and he
projected his own feelings of rejection and anger on to Beth;
Beth's reactions only confirmed his suspicions of Beth's
possessiveness of and attachment to Arlene. He treated her
as a rival.

Women's friendships and their dependency on one another do not detract from the intimacy in a sexual relationship. On the contrary, it seems that interdependent friendships aid the success and longevity of sexual relationships.
They do so by diffusing some of the intensity of a marriage
or committed sexual relationship, by providing alternative
objects for transference and by spreading the burden of
need: because women friends are able to give each other
emotional nurturance and contact, women can feel 'fed' by
their friends and not look only to their men for fulfilment.
This brings less pressure to men in relationships. In other

words, girlfriends help each other to stay in heterosexual relationships.

Daisy and Linda had been friends since school. They were the best of friends through college and afterwards, when each of them got married. They introduced their husbands, who subsequently developed a friendship. The four of them spent a lot of time together and the women continued to have lots of separate contact. After six years of marriage, and having had a daughter, Daisy and her husband split up. It was a difficult time for her, and Linda was very nurturing and caring. Daisy and her daughter Elsa spent lots of time at Linda's house with Linda and Jerry. Two years later Linda and her husband got divorced. In a similar fashion Daisy helped Linda get through the pain and loss. She kept her company a lot and shared with her the feelings she had during her divorce, reassuring Linda that the difficult time and the pain would end. They began to spend more and more time together because once again they were both single and had so much in common. They rented a beach-house together for their summer holiday, took a winter skiing trip together, and Linda cared for Elsa often so that Daisy could have some time on her own. They saw each other at least one evening a week and spoke on the phone several times a week. They both dated and had many giggles as well as angry cries about men and sex. Then Daisy met Rhonda. They were very attracted to one another and began to have a sexual relationship. This was the first sexual relationship that Daisy had had with a woman and she felt terrific excitement about this new event in her life. She felt the promise of a satisfying relationship at last and was completely enthralled by this new feeling that she didn't need to look to a man for her intimate and sexual life. Linda tried to be enthusiastic and happy for Daisy but she felt disturbed. She hated the feelings inside her because she knew that if Daisy had become involved with a man she would have dealt with it better. She felt jealous of the time and the intimacy between Daisy and Rhonda, but she tried as best she could to hold these feelings inside and to act calmly. At first Daisy and Linda continued to meet once a week for dinner. Something did not feel right between them but they each tried to carry on as if everything was fine. Then one week Linda cancelled their date, and then one evening Daisy did. Their phone calls became less frequent and Daisy began to feel annoyed with Linda because it seemed that, when they did speak or get together, Linda was depressed and behaved oddly towards her. Daisy talked to Rhonda about this and, even though they both thought that Linda might be having problems with Daisy being a lesbian, Daisy felt that it was Linda's struggle and that there was little that she could do about it.

When Daisy and Linda's lives were on a similar course — i.e., either they were both in other relationships or they were both 'single' — things worked very well between them. When Daisy became involved with Rhonda there were several significant psychological jolts in the situation. First of all Linda felt abandoned. She felt the loss of her close ties with Daisy. In addition she felt rejected and on an unconscious level became convinced that there was something lacking in her that contributed to Daisy's seeking this attachment. These feelings were heightened because Daisy's new lover was a woman. Where Linda could have 'accepted' that a man had something else to offer Daisy and thereby could have distanced her sense of abandonment and rejection, she could less easily do this when there was another woman involved. Also, she was unconsciously frightened by Daisy's lesbianism because it highlighted the fact that they were different people. Difference implied distance. Linda worried that, if she and Daisy were really separate and so different, they would not be able to remain involved with one another. Daisy, on the other hand, unconsciously felt as if she had done something wrong, as if she had betrayed Linda by having this other intimate relationship with a woman. She felt guilty about having a good relationship when she knew that Linda was lonely and unhappy because she was not involved with anyone at that time. She sensed that she had to distance herself from Linda in order to 'keep' what she now had and wanted. Having something good in her life felt as if she were hurting and betraying her close friend. Why couldn't Linda and Daisy continue to love one another and be the closest of friends? Why couldn't Linda be happy for Daisy and at the same time secure in her own attachment to Daisy? Why did Daisy feel guilty and sneaky about having what she wanted and that which made her happy? Why was it that her best friend had to be the person who seemed to want to prevent her from experiencing this happiness? If we look back to Chapter 2 and remember the young girl's experience of intimacy and loss of nurturance, we find the answers. If women must cling to one another to fill up the emptiness inside them, and if women friends unconsciously act towards one another as if they were each other's mothers, then autonomy, separateness and fulfilment in a friend will indeed feel threatening to one's sense of self and well-being.

There's been a new development in recent years in this arena of competition between women friends. Whereas it used to be, and still is for many people, that women looked to a man in order to define who she was in the world, now women are more involved in developing themselves and their own position in society. When opportunities were fewer for women and when it was economically more possible to have only one adult working to support the family, many more women were housewives and mothers and did not have paid work outside the home. This economic dependence meant that to a large extent women's identity was derived from that of their husbands — in terms of both wealth and social status. Therefore, women's competitive feelings centred on how their husbands compared to other men. There is currently a shift towards women becoming more competitive with each other. As women's social position changes and more and more women develop aspects of themselves that were previously dormant, and as women become more confident and successful outside the home, women's competitive feelings towards one another

also take on new significance. Although ultimately we know
that these feelings get in the way of women's friendships and
in many ways hold women back from developing, we can't
help but see these changes as a progressive step in the
changing role of women. For women are now seeing each
other and themselves, perhaps, with clearer definition. A
woman is seen to be a person in her own right, rather than
one who is judged according to her husband's status.
Whether or not women will display competitive behaviour
professionally and follow in the footsteps of men, as it were,
is yet to be seen. The important struggle women face is to
develop themselves and to encourage their friends in their
own attempts towards self-development.

One major social advance the women's movement has
made in the past few years has been to encourage women's
attempts to support each other in developing their strengths.
This is truly a revolutionary phenomenon, but it is still too
new a phenomenon to predict what fruits it will bring.
Supporting a friend in getting what she needs, in helping her
to be more fulfilled, assertive and strong, is an act of love
which, because of women's history and psychologies, requires a conscious struggle. For a woman to feel proud of
her friend because she looks beautiful or is making great
strides in her work life, rather than feeling competitive and
abandoned, is no minor achievement. For a woman to feel
optimistic about the possibilities in her own life rather than
unconsciously predicting inevitable deprivation and failure
is not insignificant. For a woman to accept that it is possible
for a friend to love more than one person, and to recognize
the emotional dependency she has on her friends, as well as
on her lover, is of major consequence.

When women provide support and encouragement to
each other, it may be possible to repair some of the damage
and deprivation that women have internalized. Because
most women in a patriarchal society come to feel less than
good about themselves, it is often impossible for mothers to
transmit a sense of encouragement and confidence to their
daughters. This is shifting, and hopefully we will be seeing

significant changes even within this next generation of girls. Our mothers had less of an opportunity of experiencing the nurturance and support for self-development and autonomy than our daughters do. Recognizing women's dependency on each other as well as recognizing what women are able to give to one another is a critical determining factor in the changing psychology of girls and women.

8

New Directions

We hope that, in the preceding chapters, we've begun to answer the question 'What *do* women want?' Posing this question has opened up the essential issue of emotional dependency in our early development and in adult life. From our first relationship with our mother, through our friendships and love affairs, emotional dependency and contact is the food that nourishes us. Women and men alike need to have their dependency needs met. Knowing that one can rely on others for understanding and emotional support allows one to exploit one's opportunities in a confident and expressive way. But for these dependency needs to be met we know that the ways we relate now must shift.

The current state of affairs vis-à-vis family life, heterosexuality, sexual politics, intimate relationships, child-rearing and psychological development cry out for attention and change. The extent to which people experience difficulties in their intimate relationships both with lovers and friends tells us that all is not right. At the same time some of the threads *are* right because, as most of us know, there is enormous pleasure to be had from those moments when our relationships with friends and lovers work. We appreciate how essential it is to be involved with people we like and love and can talk to and share experiences with. We know our wants and longings, and we know the pain of disappointment and rejection.

Some people look to their work for their primary source of gratification and commitment. Work and related activities are expressions of human life. They are achievements and celebrations of our potentialities. We are a social species —

that is, we need one another to survive. Although other aspects of our lives are essential they cannot replace relationships. This is a fact that we rarely sit down and spend time thinking about. Someone living in isolation and outside the milieu of social relations would not be a true human being. They might resemble a human being genetically but their capacity to think, feel, express themselves and experience the world would not be anything like what we call human.

This draws attention to two things. First, our relationships and the emotional and psychological dynamics that make up our relationships *do* warrant our time and attention. Second, as human beings we have the ability to change conditions of our lives when we understand that they need changing. We study history, we analyse the changes that we see and we try to understand why those particular changes came about. We learn from history and from our day-to-day lives in what new directions we need to be aiming. We often feel lost and swamped by the enormity of it all (and this confusion is becoming more widespread) but we continue to search for progressive and sane social directions. Over the last twelve years the women's liberation movement has uncovered some areas that need changing and changes have been and continue to be made. With change, new forms emerge and with them additional stumbling blocks present themselves and we find new ways to overcome them. Changes, on the scale we're talking about, take a long time and are often so gradual that they are difficult to pinpoint. But nothing ever stands still.

Most of the theory about psychological development has only emerged over the last hundred years, and people are learning more each day about the way our personalities develop and how we come to be who we are. It is only relatively recently that post-Freudian schools of psychoanalysis have turned their attention to the mother-infant relationship as the key to personality development. We can't help but stress the newness of all this knowledge.

It is only in the last decade that new ways of thinking

about the lives of women and their second-class status in a
patriarchal society have gained popular currency. Feminism
has much to offer to psychoanalytic thinking. Feminism
insists that we must understand the social structure of child-
rearing and how it affects men and women's psychological
development. We can no longer merely blame mothers for
their children's shortcomings and leave it at that. Blaming
mothers is a short-hand. Such a course produces only a
partial explanation. One might just as well blame fathers for
their absence. Both of these attitudes would be to miss the
point. Every time a psychologist identifies the mother as the
cause of problems, it is, *in fact*, an indictment of our society's
arrangements for child-rearing. Women are restricted by
their social role. If we blind ourselves to this, we substitute
blaming the woman for true understanding.

What we must do now is to put attention and energy into
making progressive changes in our daily lives. These
changes will aim to alleviate the imbalances that women and
men experience in their psychological development. We
certainly have enough information to tell us that both
women and men suffer under the present constructions. As
social beings we will create new ways.

In fact, a social revolution concerning relations between
the sexes and child-rearing practices is now in process. The
institution of the family is in flux.[1] In Britain, one third of marriages end in divorce, one quarter of households are headed
by women (and the figure is rising), homosexuality is more
openly accepted and many people are deciding not to have
babies. At the same time, there has been a burgeoning of
alternative ways of living and of bringing up children. Some
of these have been conscious experiments, deliberate rejections of the nuclear family, while others have come about
from force of circumstance and a breaking down of the old

1. The family has been in flux for the last six hundred years. See, for
    example: Philippe Aries, *Centuries of Childhood*, New York 1973;
    Elizabeth Badinter, *Mother Love*, New York 1981; Edward Shorter,
    The Making of the Modern Family, New York 1975.

ways. As new lifestyles, whatever their cause, are forged, the people involved are engaged in a process in which their expectations, their unconscious ideas, their prejudices and their aspirations interact in complicated ways. Psychological change cannot be forced. It needs a framework within which to develop, and an environment in which the resistance and the difficulties women and men encounter can be overcome. Individuals trying to raise their children outside the conventional norm, and couples and new family groupings working out alternative lifestyles, suffer a double difficulty. They have to face their internal reluctance to change in a context in which they will not be receiving support from the outside world. The heterosexual nuclear family receives tremendous psychological and political support in our system in both subtle and overt ways; people who do not conform suffer many disadvantages. Nevertheless, that has not prevented thousands and thousands of people from experimenting with new ways of living and raising children.

We know that different methods of child rearing can be put into practice and that mothering as we now know it is not fixed and inevitable. Just forty years ago, during the Second World War, the state instituted nursery provisions for children so that mothers would be free to carry out the work that their fighting husbands had left behind. The ideological thrust in that period was to persuade mothers that communal child care was beneficial at the same time as it allowed them to perform the highest service: a contribution to the war effort. After the war women were beamed a different ideological message: give us back our wives and sweethearts. The nurseries were closed and women moved out of the essential productive industries back into the household. When a whole society is geared to change such as this, the possibilities seem endless and exciting. That is why we personally feel so positive about rethinking sexual relations and child-rearing practices from a perspective that sees the sexual politics of the situation. We also feel that the shifts and experiments occurring now highlight the urgency

for change. So many people are no longer able to live within
the old structures and are seeking new arrangements.
Among the possibilities that exist in cities and towns
throughout the United Kingdom today are communes,
cooperatives, shared parenting by heterosexual couples,
shared parenting by lesbian mothers, fathers raising children
without partners, together with kindergarten and nursery
facilities run on non-sexist lines and including male as well as
female staff.

One cannot judge the results of these experiments in a
particularly coherent way because each experiment has a
slightly different orientation. Although there aren't many
communes relative to the general population, they exist as a
significant force, as a reaction to dissatisfactions in the
traditional nuclear family. In some of the communes there
has been a desire to get away from sex-role stereotyping, in
others the thrust has been towards '60s values of support,
honesty, free love, and so on. In such communes, the
relationship of women to child-rearing, domestic labour and
emotional life may mirror a woman's lot outside the
commune. The struggles that a commune face and the way
in which it takes up issues of sexual politics will reflect the
commitment and consciousness of the members. In some
communes which are dedicated to sexual equality within the
commune, to child care by all members, to cooking rotas
and joint cleaning schemes, there is a resistance to sharing
the emotional life of the commune. The women continue to
be responsible for emotional processing and refuelling.
In a spirit of anti-individualism, the emotional life of the
commune is tacitly buried and emerges in a contemporary
form of 'women's work'.

It is in smaller units that we are seeing the most dramatic
changes in the last few years. Many couples who have
children together now have been forced by economic circumstances to think about and arrange parenting differently
from in the past. Other couples, heterosexual and homosexual, have decided to share the parenting, to seek employ-
ment that makes that possible. Many women have been

deciding to have children on their own, and many people are involved in intimate sexual relationships without living together. In all these arrangements, the issue of emotional dependency is on the table even if it is not squarely addressed. Each one of these challenges stirs up emotional issues in a new way and demands new responses and adaptations. The hidden dependency transactions that we have been discussing between women and men need to be understood and grappled with in new contexts. We are at a crossroads.

Many of us will shy away from the tasks that need to be done because they feel insurmountable or because it is hard to know where to start. Society is often negative or defensive about change. Some people will avoid confronting the question of emotional nurturing, seeing it as a diversion from the need for a broad economic revolution that in its wake will usher in the equality of women, men and children. But economic revolutions up to the present have not seen it as a priority to challenge the relations of the sexes at more than an economic level. Although economic changes are progressive, they are only a step — an essential one — in the process of achieving equity. This book seeks to challenge the power relations between women and men. We need to uncover our prejudices, our resistances and the unconscious structures which shape our actions, and that make change so very difficult. As we identify and come to understand these hidden forces, we will be able to approach the present struggle more openly and seriously. To change attitudes about ourselves and towards each other requires hard and painful work; changing our behaviour is even more difficult. It needs conscious effort and a willingness to be vulnerable and exposed in ways which we have not known before. Men living with feminists have felt the effects of some of these demands. Women themselves have realized the need for support from other women and have met in consciousness-raising groups to discuss the meaning and the effects of being raised as girls. Men have also been joining consciousness-raising groups, not in as large numbers and usually not with such a broad scope. And in fact, in several men's groups, emotional issues are rarely touched on. The most interesting of the groups we have heard about concentrates on the topic of fatherhood and its meaning in men's lives. So, although the experiments we are talking about are taking place in individual households, there are support groups, women's groups, fathers' groups, couples' groups, and so on, that are involved in processing the social revolution we are part of. This consciousness and support are important features of the struggle we are involved in because they make social activities which can so easily be experienced as individual.

Our analysis leads us to argue that one of the tasks in front of men at this point is for them to recognize their dependency on women, to take responsibility for it and for women to accept it openly. Through these pages we have met many men who are in flight from any recognition of their dependency needs. They take comfort in the more obvious dependency of their female partners, unaware of how their own dependency needs would be apparent if women showed more self-sufficiency and did not carry the dependency.

Jane and Saul were committed to struggling against this traditional scenario and tried to overcome the obstacles to intimacy that cropped up between them. They noticed that they had a tendency to live on an emotional seesaw. From time to time Jane would feel depressed and at a loss. Saul would appear to be the strong one, capable of maintaining his stability and being secure. Then Jane would assert her self-sufficiency. Saul's self-doubts and feelings of inadequacy would surface, culminating in a fear that Jane would leave him. Having lived through these backs and forths several times, they both undertook to try something new. They confronted the possibility that this was the only way their relationship could work. Perhaps they had to live in a situation where one person was okay and the other collapsing? Perhaps this was the only way they knew how to get attention and contact. They realized that they both relied

on a self-image that embodied the rescuer who was im-
pervious and strong. In other words, they were both in
retreat from their vulnerable, insecure, worrying selves. If
Jane was emotionally fed up, not only could Saul feel his
strength in taking care of her but also his relative strength
was temporarily boosted by seeing her state, for into it he
unconsciously projected his own distress, thereby divorcing
himself from it. When Saul was feeling lousy, Jane, relieved
that he too could be insecure in the relationship, would
comfort him and come to feel in good form herself. As they
struggled together over this dynamic and realized in effect
that they had encapsulated their needs in a package which
they passed between them, they decided to try a new
equilibrium. Each of them would recognize their dependency on each other, their need for each other's nurturance and care and their need for reassurance that they
weren't about to be left. Saul found this hard to do. He
winced at having to face his dependency on Jane when he
was feeling good in himself. It seemed to him weak and as
though he were giving up something. Jane had an internal
struggle to face in relation to Saul's exposure of this part of
himself, for, without realizing it, she had projected on to him
her need to see him as strong and invulnerable. Much as a
part of her wanted him to be more open, she didn't take
readily to his expression of his dependency. From the
outside, the emotional seesaw in Jane and Saul's relationship
might be mistaken for a kind of equality between the two of
them. But the struggles in which they had to engage in
coming to terms with their dependency needs were not, as
we can see, symmetrical.

At the same time Jane tried to stop undervaluing herself
and her competence. She tried to integrate the needy part of
herself with her accomplished self. When she did this she felt
that Saul still ignored her difficulties and only related to her
strengths. She felt she had to persuade him that she could be
needy and competent at the same time, only half believing it
herself. He didn't know exactly what this meant or how he
should come to terms with it. If Jane had an aggravating

phone call with her mother (with whom she had a very strained and dreadful relationship), he didn't know whether to ask more about it, commiserate or discuss it. He felt helpless to make her feel better. And so he would stay silent. She would interpret this quietness as lack of interest and feel abandoned. In fact, Saul simply did not know what she wanted. 'What *do* women want, after all?' He didn't know what it meant to provide nurturance on a day-to-day basis. When he could tell Jane this, she was relieved and replied that she wasn't needing to be rescued, she wasn't needing solutions; she was needing his understanding and attention. She told him he didn't need to have answers or interpretations, but that she would appreciate a hug and some questions. She'd like him to try and get into her shoes just for a minute to see what she was going through and then step out of them and relate to her with tenderness and understanding.

Saul's willingness to expose his unknowingness, rather than withdrawing, was an example of his taking responsibility for aspects of their emotional life together. He was struggling against his desire to give up and not bother to learn the skill of relating in this way. He felt he was learning a new language without quite understanding the grammar, and so he didn't know when he was doing it right or when he was doing it wrong. Slowly, he came to be able to react spontaneously, but only after tremendous efforts.

When Jane had a report to write for work she would get very nervous. She was sure she couldn't do it and would work herself up into a terrible state. She longed for Saul to do it for her because such things seemed so easy for him. She hated herself for going through these traumas every few months. Usually she did rope Saul into doing some part of it, even if it was just the opening or concluding paragraph.

This time, when Jane started to get uptight as the deadline for producing the paper neared, Saul calmly reminded her that she always managed to do the papers in the end, and that they were always clear and well written. He said this to her with an attitude that conveyed a sense that she could do it. He wasn't in any way pushing her away, or taking over for her; he was recognizing her anxiety and not dismissing it, while not being overwhelmed by it himself. He was able to see both her competence and her worries. He said he would sit with her in the study while she got started; he had work to do and would be at the other end of the long desk they shared. Jane settled herself down to the report and, although she would feel waves of panic rising up in her, she determined not to let them immobilize her, because, as Saul had pointed out, she always did do her reports, and she wasn't going to renege this time. She did the whole report and realized that she didn't need the odd paragraph from Saul. She had done it all herself. His help had been crucial in getting her over the first hump. With his confidence she was able to complete the task herself.

When they talked about this incident, Jane said that she felt pleased with herself for not having got into a terrible state. She was having a hard time giving up the idea that writing reports and the like was a scary experience that generated tremendous anxiety. She was used to approaching writing with incredible drama, as though all of her life were on the line in that activity. But on this occasion she had really changed that experience. She saw that Saul had really given her something. He had sensed her difficulty and, instead of trying to push her or persuade her that she could do it, he was able to give her a confidence in herself. This was unusual on his part because in the past, when he could bear her anxiety no more, he would either get angry with her and go off or he would go over the proposed content and structure of the report again and again with her. In both responses he would feel irritated, although the latter boosted his own feelings of adequacy and competence. This time, he was able to give her what *she* needed, not more and not less. He related to her as a separate and capable person. His giving to her in this way allowed her to make some changes inside herself, and they were both able to enjoy the giving and receiving.

In the course of their relationship they recognized their dependency on each other and the separate needs that each of them had. This created a slight chink in the merger between the two of them so that they were better able to see where each of them began and ended emotionally. They tried not to be emotional flagbearers for each other but took up instead their own issues and brought them to each other. In the course of talking about the changes in their relationship they both expressed how much more equal they felt it had become. Just as they were both sharing responsibility for the household labour, so they shared the responsibility for keeping the relationship and their needs within it afloat. Saul had occasional twinges of discomfort and embarrassment about always trying to look at his vulnerabilities rather than coping with them in the old ways, but it was a relatively small price compared to what he felt he got out of being involved in a much more conscious and equal emotional exchange. Sometimes he would feel alienated from other men, particularly those at work who seemed so intent on bolstering their macho images and denying their vulnerabilities, but in his men's groups he found support and comradeship. Other men in the group discussed how hard they had found the idea of not providing economically for their women. Although they thought that this attitude was outmoded, the notion that the women they were involved with contributed to their own support was disconcerting. For some men, of course, this was experienced as straightforward relief. It removed the 'burden' of having to be the provider. For most of the men in the group, though, a variety of the following attitudes came up. 'If I'm not supporting her, then I don't exactly know what or how to give.' 'If she can support herself and make as much as me then maybe she'll be more likely to leave me.' 'If I don't support her economically, it makes her much more of an equal and I'm frightened of that.' Because the group had a commitment to work through these attitudes and it understood the patriarchal structure that motivated such sexist sentiments, the men were not afraid to speak their minds and were able to look behind the attitudes to the much deeper feelings they represented.

All the men in the group were able to face the fact that they were really quite scared of women and that deep down women's equality, and separateness especially, made them uneasy. In all of their relationships, whether at work or at home, they noticed the ease with which they would obscure that fact from themselves. They did this in a curious way, either by mythologizing women in one way or another or devaluing them. The men began to face their fear of women, especially the worry that if they opened up they would be engulfed. They examined the ideas they had acquired in their upbringing about women 'wanting everything', 'it's never enough', 'don't give in', and so on and began to see these as defensive expressions learned in the male culture. They reflected on the paradoxical attitudes they had absorbed in relation to women. How was it that the weaker sex was potentially so very powerful? They wondered why they were so terribly afraid of letting their guard down with women, when at the same time it was only with women that they felt free to let their vulnerabilities show. While they most often talked about themselves in relation to work, ambition and competition, they returned time and again to the theme of their fear and confusion about women. All of them were able to discuss the occasional irrational rage and contemptuous attitudes that surfaced in them and how these attitudes often covered up other feelings. Several of the men felt threatened by the ease with which their partners would talk openly with their girlfriends about emotional issues of one kind and another. The buzzing conversation in the kitchen could be dismissed in one way as 'just women's talk', but they came to see that such a dismissal itself embodies a defensive attitude predicated on envy and exclusion.

Monika's struggle with Carlo over the cooking and the dishes shows us another side of the psychological difficulties we are choosing to take on when we try to change the domestic arrangements. Carlo was a first-generation Italian-American. He had grown up in a household in which the men never entered the kitchen but awaited service. He had come a long way from that himself. He had met Monika at university where they were both studying for their Ph.Ds in history. He respected her a lot and had no difficulty seeing her as an intellectual equal. Although they did not live together, they spent about five nights a week together at her house. He would leave his books and papers there and Monika found herself getting irritated by this and the fact that he didn't keep the things he left at her house in neater piles. She didn't feel that she had grounds for saying very much about the situation though, because she liked Carlo's staying. She did, however, notice how resentful she was that Carlo never helped out in the kitchen when she cooked. Eventually she brought this up with him in the context of a conversation they were having about feminism in the nineteenth century. She said that she thought he took her cooking for granted and wished that he could acknowledge the giving in some way. He immediately felt embarrassed and said that he would do the dishes. Monika accepted but when they cleared off the table at the end of the meal she noticed that Carlo picked up the Ajax to do the dishes with. At first she thought this was really funny, but then she realized that he really didn't have a clue how to go about clearing up; he had never learned. As she put away the things in the kitchen, she could see what problems he was having out of the corner of her eye. Unfortunately for both of them, he was making a lousy job of it and Monika burst in and said, 'Oh, for Christ's sake, go in the other room, I'll do it.' She interrupted the process of his learning how to do this household task because she couldn't give up the control and watch him doing it badly. This tiny incident illustrates just how difficult these kinds of changes which look so small on the outside can be. Carlo did feel it was unmanly to wash the supper dishes although he knew that was a ridiculous attitude. He didn't really see why Monika was making a fuss and why she couldn't take these things in her stride; after all, they weren't living together and he didn't really see why he should be nagged at about his belongings or the housework. It was this attitude that he brought to the dishes and it made him approach the job unenthusiastically and without much concentration. He assumed it would be quite easy and did not understand when Monika pushed him away from the sink. For Monika, so used to doing the dishes on her own, it was hard to give way to someone else who did them badly and unwillingly. She wasn't able to contain her own feelings of needing to control when Carlo was in front of the sink, and before she knew what had happened she had intervened and played along with the very situation that she had wanted to change. Carlo responded by proposing they eat out. He felt guilty that Monika was giving to him when she didn't want to. He had a hard time hearing that that *wasn't* Monika's experience and that she liked giving to him but that she wanted the giving acknowledged. He took her request for acknowledgement as an accusation of sexism and as a warning that he shouldn't have Monika do anything for him. In reality she was very happy to cook for him as long as this did not go unrecognized. One day Carlo decided he wanted to cook a meal at Monika's. Remembering how intolerant she had been over the dishes incident, she promised herself she wouldn't intervene and try and control the whole cooking operation. She offered to be a kitchen help, cleaning the vegetables etc., but pretty soon she realized that it made her anxious to watch him trying to cook. He only had a very approximate idea about how he was supposed to go about things and had chosen a fairly elaborate dish out of the cookbook. Monika felt her impulse to take over, but reminded herself of her promise to herself and went into the living room to read. She found it excruciating to imagine what was going on in the kitchen and not be involved and was shocked by just how hard it was to give up something that she knew how to do so easily. Eventually, to distract herself, she went out on an errand to buy flowers and wine to go with the meal.

Through these two incidents, Monika had to confront just how little she trusted Carlo to be able to do something that was previously in her sphere of competence. Even though it wasn't an enormous issue, it highlighted a dynamic that is

often present between women and men. The woman feels
desperately that she wants to be given to, or that she wants
the domestic arrangements to change, but she has become so
used to her way of doing things or so unused to receiving,
that disengaging from the process and letting the other
person take a new role was very hard.

Joshua and Rebecca made a commitment to raising their
child together. They had decided that the only way to break
the sex-role stereotyped ideas that a child takes in would be
to provide the child from its first day with an environment in
which they participated equally. They were both university
teachers and so their schedule was a lot more flexible than
most. They felt they had an advantage over their friends for
they would not have to take half-time jobs and reduce their
living standards in order for both of them to be fully
involved in parenting. They could approach joint parenting
with extremely good conditions and they didn't really
envisage any problems. Before the baby arrived, they
discussed some of their fears and fantasies. Rebecca worried
about whether the baby would think she were still special if
she weren't constantly present. Joshua talked about being
scared of the tininess of the baby and feeling clumsy,
worrying that he would only have theories about how to stop
it crying without really knowing how to soothe it. When
Rebecca went into labour, Joshua was with her and stayed
with her throughout the delivery. The experience was an
ecstatic one for the two of them and they felt very close and
happy. When they brought the baby home from the hospital
they were determined to be equally involved. They had
noticed that their friends who started off with the same
intentions were having a more or less difficult time keeping
to that commitment. Economic factors intervened in John
and Mary's relationship when John was offered a job with a
TV company; John was flattered and felt he couldn't turn
down either the opportunity or the money. Mary found
herself alone with the baby most of the time and, since she
couldn't find anyone to look after the baby for the time John

was meant to put in, she delayed going back to work for another few months and then eventually gave up her part-time job altogether. John was not very eager to look after the baby when he came home, and Mary, feeling somewhat resentful of his ability to breeze in and out of child care when he could manage it, kept the baby near to her, thus reinforcing the sense that John had that he didn't know how to relate to it for more than a few minutes at a time.

Other friends had other versions of the same story and seeing this around them made Joshua and Rebecca very wary of not making the same mistakes. Their baby was born at the beginning of the long summer vacation so they both had three months of time free of classes and formal work commitments. For the first few weeks they both seemed to spend all of their time with the baby, they were both reluctant to leave the house for very long and were caught up in responding to Shanna's needs. They both felt good about their participation and as the baby moved into her second month, one or other of them would go off for several hours at a time, confident that the other parent would be able to interpret the meaning of the baby's various cries and gurgles. Termtime came around again and Joshua went off to his office to advise his students. He took the baby with him on this occasion as they had now devised a scheme for when each of them would look after her based on their schedules. Rebecca remembers watching Joshua prepare Shanna for the trip, wrapping her up, taking along a bottle and various toys for her to play with, but neglecting to take nappies or the cream for nappy rash. At that moment, Rebecca was aware of a fear that she thought had been worked through. She felt her distrust of Joshua's ability to be a good caretaker. She had felt tempted to pack up all the things that Shanna would need for the few hours but had steeled herself against doing this, telling herself that such an act was controlling and not necessarily considerate. Joshua might feel insulted or undermined. Rebecca felt quite torn inside but they worked very hard in their relationship to avoid making the kind of sexist assumptions that we all make almost automatically, and packing Shanna's things up would have implied that Joshua was 'helping' her out rather than shouldering his responsibility. Rebecca held back from her impulse to push nappies in the bag and put up with the complicated feelings stirred up in her when Joshua went out of the door with Shanna, underequipped.

About an hour later Joshua rushed into the house to pick up some nappies. The college was situated on a campus, so the nearest place to replenish supplies was home. Later that day they talked about what had happened. Joshua said how pissed off he was with himself for not being 100% on top of the situation and at the ways in which he relied on Rebecca to take care of the details. Forgetting the nappies had brought up a momentary reaction that he didn't really want to be doing all this child care. He felt able to accept the feeling in himself, not judge himself for being that way, and get a grip on the situation again. When Rebecca told him that she had noticed that he had left without nappies, he was at first annoyed, but when she explained what a hard internal tussle she had had to leave the situation that way, he saw all the ramifications and was grateful. They both felt that they had made a significant step forward in terms of trying to be joint parents. Rebecca had to give up control, and Joshua saw that if he wasn't alert in the detailed kind of way he needed to be, he would be giving less than adequate care. If Rebecca had just stepped in and righted the situation, he would not have begun developing those skills normally associated with femininity, like attention to detail.

This struggle was one which came up in various forms through Shanna's infancy. Once, when Joshua was working intently on a paper with a colleague, Shanna was making a lot of noise in the other room. He was so engrossed in his work that he couldn't really tear himself away to see what exactly Shanna was wanting. He kept giving her juice and when she cried again, more juice. When Rebecca came home a couple of hours later, she noticed that Shanna's nappy was really soaked. Joshua hadn't realized that some of the crying was as a result of the wet nappy, caused by so much fluid. It wasn't a major disaster, but it reminded Joshua of how fathering in the way he was committed to doing it was much more than a custodial role. That being available to Shanna meant that, if he were working hard, he would have to learn to take short bursts of time off to be attentive to her. With such incidents, Rebecca had to struggle with herself against a prejudiced notion that she knew best, that she and Joshua were making a mistake about all this, maybe they had gone out on a limb, etc. These thoughts occurred only infrequently, for most of the time she was aware of the difference between her life and that of her friends. She found that Joshua's participation meant that she could still be involved with things at work that interested her. Although she wasn't getting much sleep these days, she felt very good in herself. She felt close to Joshua and really valued the shared parenting; she loved time with Shanna and rarely felt short-tempered, and she maintained a reasonably lively interest in the outer world. She became an example to her friends who were starting to have children, who had been discouraged by the difficulties others in the circle committed to joint child-rearing had encountered. When Shanna joined the day-care centre at the university, the staff there commented on how little separation anxiety she seemed to exhibit in the morning and the relative ease with which she took to other adults. We can speculate that Shanna's internal world meant that she could approach situations with much less anxiety than some of the other children. Shanna was the recipient of the consistent attention of two parents who were more or less unambivalent about spending lots of time with her. Child-rearing was for both of them an additional joy in their lives and both of them were able to meet her basic needs without too many problems and convey a confidence that things were all right with the world. Because Rebecca and Joshua both had other activities in their lives and because they felt supported by each other's care for Shanna, they were able to come to the nurturing situation not looking for Shanna to fill a void in their own lives or to be a representation of the parts of themselves that were unfulfilled. Shanna was very treasured and in this sense was a vehicle for much of their love, but they also learned to establish the boundaries that were necessary for her to consolidate a sense of self based on strength, rather than based on a disappointment with and a flight from the early dependent period as we have seen in other cases.

In communes, different struggles are taking place over similar issues. Some parents are having to fight against treating their children as their sole responsibility and work through the insecurity that entrusting them with other adults brings. Commune members are making every effort to provide a stable environment for the first few years of a particular child's life so that the extended parenting that is offered is not just transitory. For it is very hard for a mother to overcome her possessiveness and distrust of others' interest in a child if the membership of the living circle except for her and the child is in a state of flux. Children raised in stable circumstances in communes seem to have a very good chance of getting their dependency needs met when they are very young, for communes provide a structure of parenting that is fundamentally different from the 'traditional' one that makes it so hard for our mothers to give us the kind of care we crave. Of course, the unconscious attitudes that are conveyed to children about gender and about parenting do not disappear within one generation, but the foundations for change are being laid.

We ourselves have some ideas about what things might look like in the future. In this book we have offered a description of the way dependency operates in our friendships and intimate relationships. At the risk of being called idealistic we'd like to offer a different picture — a possibility of another way.

Imagining the world three generations from now opens up mind-boggling possibilities. The structure of the world economy will no doubt be radically transformed. The anatomy of each country and society will look very different. The conventional family unit as we know it may have almost entirely disappeared and therefore child-rearing arrangements will be very different from what they are today. In order to describe a new psychology we must focus on the life of a newborn girl and boy and the parenting they receive. Let us, therefore, imagine a setting that is somewhat familiar to us. That is, a family grouping of a woman, man and their children. In our looking towards new directions for child-rearing, a pivotal point is equal and shared parenting by both men and women. As we have described throughout the book, there is currently a severe imbalance in the lives of women and men, with women, even if they have jobs, still involved primarily in the world of child-rearing and domestic life, whilst men are raised to be so outer-directed and achievement-oriented that their abilities to be emotionally giving, nurturing and vulnerable are harshly curtailed. This imbalance with women in the home and men in the world must be changed if there is to be a change in the psychologies of the coming generations of girls and boys. A new balance must be created in which both women and men participate in the world inside the home as well as the world outside. Both women and men must continue to develop themselves in areas of work and interest. Both must be able to feel confident, substantive and capable in the world. At the same time, both must come to feel emotionally integrated and capable of expressing and receiving love and care. Both must be capable of a positive awareness of themselves, defined within boundaries, so that they can relate to others from a position of security and self-love. We have seen in earlier chapters how men's and women's present psychological make-up makes it extremely difficult, if not nearly impossible, for them to relate to one another in that kind of way.

In the new society, both women and men must continue to grow and develop throughout their lifetimes because of their involvements both inside and outside the home. There will no longer be a division made between the years of a woman's life when she is devoting herself to her children and those when she returns to her own life. Women will no longer feel stifled and imprisoned by living in the world of babies

and feeling themselves losing the capacity for adult conversation and interest. Women will no longer fear being
forty and having their grown children leave them to an
empty home — an empty life, an emptiness inside.

Men will no longer be cut off from their own offspring.
Men will no longer be forced to be out in a world of
competition only to return home for a few hours each
evening. Men will no longer be strangers with a powerful
mystique whose absence has a more profound effect on
their children's psychologies than their presence.

Let us imagine a woman and a man living together and
expecting a child several generations from now, each having
part-time work outside the home in which they are engaged
and interested. Their work schedules are arranged in such a
way as to give each of them time alone with the coming
infant, time alone away from the infant, time together with
the infant and time together away from the infant. Their
baby is a son, and later they have a daughter. Let us imagine
the lives of those two children.

A boy infant is born from his mother's womb. Throughout
the pregnancy the father is involved in the preparation for
the birth. Minutes after the birth both the mother and father
have access to the infant. They each cuddle him, kiss him,
care for him. This couple has decided that breast feeding is
the most desirable form of feeding in the early months and
so they self-consciously and thoughtfully arrange for the
father to have contact with the infant more often than the
mother through bathing, cuddling, changing of nappies,
lying with and talking to his son. Milk is expressed from the
breast to a bottle for the time when the mother is away from
the infant. The infant takes in the smells, feels and sounds of
both a man and a woman equally. His father's voice and
smell is as much a comfort to him as is his mother's. In the
undifferentiated world of the infant both a man and a
woman are within his orbit. His sense of survival and utter
dependency are engaged with both a man and a woman. As
he is responded to, his trust and sense of care and love is

associated with both a man and a woman. He takes in the
caring of both his father and mother, thereby incorporating
both into his developing psychology. As the baby grows, in
his first year, he begins to differentiate himself from each of
them and each of them from the other. There are two people
who are central to his world and his sense of well-being. He
embodies aspects of each of his parents' personalities.
His sense of security is less fragile than that of previous
generations of one-parent (mother) reared children, because his survival does not depend on one person. Therefore, when he experiences upsets with his father, for
example, because his father may not respond quickly
enough at any given moment, the infant is not utterly bereft
or terrified. His inner world does not collapse with one
parent's absence because the infant's internal world and
sense of well-being rests on a second foundation. Absence of
one parent will not necessarily mean loss of self. Because the
infant's needs and sense of self are not bound up with only
one parent, his internal world is not so fragile.

As this little boy approaches his second year of life and
begins to experience his own boundaries and sense of self
apart from his parents more clearly, his psychological
separation takes place in relation to both a man and a
woman. From birth both parents have related to him as a
boy, although the definitions of masculine and feminine
have changed dramatically from present-day definitions.
The sense of oneself as male or female remains, but the
meanings of masculinity and femininity have been transformed. So, for example, being feminine includes being
assertive, confident, sure of oneself; being masculine includes being vulnerable, needy, nurturant. During his first
steps towards psychological self-definition, the boy is
encouraged to identify positively with his father. At this
point the little boy embodies aspects of both parents and as
he separates he takes with him, so to speak, part of each of
them. He no longer has to define himself as *not* like his
mother, his primary caretaker, in order to know himself as a
boy, as did generations of boys before him. He does not

have to cut off or repress the 'feminine' parts of himself at this early age. He has taken in aspects of a mother who is feminine, but the feminine will no longer be weak, fragile, soft, needy, a comforter only. Feminine will also mean clearly defined, nurturant, containing, strong, creative. In his developing sense of self and gender identity, the boy will be able to take with him aspects of his mother while at the same time identifying with a father who is nurturant, emotionally available, reliable in his presence and caretaking. His psychological development and separation will be a process of integration rather than splitting-off and repressing.

As he grows, the boy will not come to feel ashamed or humiliated by emotional vulnerability. He will come to feel that emotions are human, not exclusively feminine, and he will be encouraged to express his own feelings as well as to be aware of others'. He will be learning from both his parents (as well as from teachers, friends, books, etc.) the skills of nurturance. He will learn how to listen to others and how to respond in a caring manner. He will observe his father doing these things and will interpret them as being a part of what it means to become a man.

Because he was raised by both parents he will come to have a different way of thinking about women, both consciously and unconsciously. He will no longer fear women's power or unconsciously think of them as witches or magicians. As he grows into a man he will not be unconsciously terrified by women who seem to have the power to control or possess him. He will not fear losing himself in a heterosexual relationship. He will not need the defences to keep women out which men today need. Because he is raised to learn caring skills he will no longer think of women as 'intuitive' because he too will have the ability to become involved with others in sensitive ways.

Because he has a mother who has work and a place in the world in which she feels competent and productive, the boy will come to be less frightened by women's needs. Not only has he developed the skills of nurturance so he feels better able to meet a woman's emotional needs, but because the woman does not look so much to him and a family for self-definition there is actually less being asked of him than in present relationships. His conscious and unconscious images of women will contain respect because women will be defined and active people who have an impact in the world. Because his own emotional dependency needs will be out in the open he will be able to appreciate the nurturing he receives. He will value it more and it will no longer be relegated to an invisible status. Through his respect and appreciation of women his psychology will be very different from that of men in previous generations whose psychological make-up included elements of misogyny.[2] This boy will become a man who feels himself to be an equal with women. The games he plays as a boy will not differ drastically from the games girls his age play. He will not be limited by sex-role stereotyped toys and books. As a man he will not feel threatened by women's autonomy in the world. He will not feel his own sense of self-worth challenged by a competent woman. He will be able to have women friends as well as lovers because he will appreciate women as people. He will not have to sexualize his relationships with women because he won't be afraid of them.

He will know how to become involved with women in ways other than sexual. He will have closer and more intimate friendships with other men because they will not have to hide their vulnerabilities from one another for fear of being weak and 'feminine'. His men friends will be able to respond and give to him in ways that in previous generations only women could. He will talk to his men and women friends about the children and domestic life as well as his other work or interests. His life will not be divided between working days on the one hand and, on the other, evenings and weekends for relaxation and family life at the same time as he worries about financial responsibility or having to achieve a certain status because he is a man. His life will be

2.   See Dorothy Dinnerstein, *The Rocking of the Cradle and the Ruling of the World*, London 1978.

more integrated and evenly balanced with work, family life
and child-rearing, friends and activities all playing important parts.

And how would the life of a daughter being born into that
family be different?

The infant girl is born of her mother's womb and, just as in
the pregnancy with her brother, father participates in the
preparations for her arrival. Just after the birth both mother
and father have equal access to her; holding her, kissing and
cuddling with her, talking to her, changing her nappies,
bathing her. She sucks at her mother's breast, but the sound of
her father's voice, his smell, his touch is all a part of her early
world. He comforts her and attends to her. He feeds her
mother's milk from a bottle. He responds to her cries and her
gurgles. In her first months of life, father and mother
surround her and she relies on them both for her comfort and
survival. During the first year of life she internalizes aspects
of both parents' personalities. She communicates with both
and her sense of well-being depends on both of them being
in her world.

As she approaches the end of her first year she begins to
separate psychologically. Each day she makes great strides
in her developing a sense of herself as separate from her
father and separate from her mother. She begins to differentiate the two of them much more clearly. Her developing
personality is an embodiment of the love and care of each of
her parents, and aspects of her own personality will come to
resemble aspects of each of their personalities. She experiences both her mother and her father going into the world
and coming back again. She is witness to a woman's ability
to be autonomous. As she begins to identify with mother
because of her shared gender, she experiences the possibilities of things to come in her own life. Each time her mother
leaves and she is with her father she learns two things. She
learns that women can go out safely into the world and
return again and she learns that men can be relied on for
emotional caretaking and survival. Her father is part of her
life in his presence rather than in his absence, in contrast with

the experience of generations of girls before her. The little girl can internalize both the outer-directed and the nurturing aspects of both parents. Her books and games do not have girls and women portrayed as household servants while men do the important work needed for family survival. Domestic life and creative, productive work outside the family will be a part of her world just as both are parts of her brother's world. She is encouraged to develop her physical strengths, and her curiosity about the things around her is not restricted. The world outside the home is a place she will have access to just as her mother does. She learns skills of nurturance and domestic work because it is a part of human activity — something that all members of the family do. Unlike generations of girls before her, she does not learn to place her own needs second, stifle herself and in place of personal fulfilment encourage and look after others. As a girl she experiences herself as an equal with boys and respects them in realistic ways. She does not hold herself back when playing games with them for fear of winning and upsetting them. She does not idealize them on the one hand and feel they need to be protected on the other. She does not feel she will suffer or be punished for her strengths. Enjoying education or doing well at school will not jeopardize her femininity. She can identify with her father in many ways and not feel that this is a betrayal of who her mother is. Both parents have things to offer her and she can use these things for her own development freely and with encouragement.

Girls who grow up with parents who are both nurturing and autonomous have the world open to them psychologically in ways that girls in previous generations didn't. Even in the 1970s, when the women's liberation movement had made some headway and girls and women had many more opportunities open to them than their mothers had, they found that psychologically they were unprepared for these opportunities. They held themselves back for fear of betraying their mothers, because of guilt feelings, fear of success and autonomy, etc. In this new generation the girl's psychological development is such that those previous constraints are no longer present. Girls growing up with mothers who are both satisfied in their active productivity or creativity in the world and who are emotionally nourished and fed will transmit an entirely different sense to their daughters of what it means to become a woman. The little girl born into the family we describe grows up feeling all kinds of possibilities are open to her. She is expected to develop herself in the fullest possible way. She is expected to be an autonomous, capable person in the world, just like her mother. She is expected to be a sexual woman and to take pleasure in her own body. She does not feel guilty about her mother's life because her mother is more satisfied and is an autonomous woman herself. She doesn't feel pain when she thinks about her mother's life — she feels pride.

The mother in our story transmits to her daughter that she can expect continued nurturance and that she will get it from men or women. The daughter witnessed her parents' relationship and sees that her father is emotionally available and nurturing. She sees a shared and equal dependency between her parents and she comes to feel that expressing her own needs with a partner later in life will be perfectly normal and safe. She will be able to choose to be in an intimate relationship with a man because he may be a desirable partner — not because she must be heterosexual. She is different from women in previous generations in that she experiences men's vulnerability and dependency as completely acceptable and normal and not some weakness in character. She will not come to feel that men are a disappointment. She will not look to a man to fill her life because she will have a secure sense of herself; she will not be looking to a man to supply a missing piece.

Similarly, because the girl has taken in care and love from both parents and deprivation is not built into her psychology, she no longer gives to others out of the well of her unmet needs. The narcissistic aspect of women's ability to give which we discussed in Chapter 2 will change. Women will have the ability and desire to give to another out of a position of completeness in their lives.

Girls will no longer experience the push-pull dynamic in their relationships with their mothers. Mothers will relate less ambivalently to their daughters because they are feeling nurtured themselves. They will not need to teach their daughters to give up the expectation of continued emotional nurturance (the push). Mothers will no longer pull their daughters to remain in a restricted domestic world because the mothers themselves will no longer feel those restrictions. A mother will encourage her daughter to enter the world, to explore, to be active, to create.

When both parents nurture and raise children, the psychological period of separation-individuation will be much easier and more successful than it presently is. There will be less tension and anger surrounding the infant because the pressures of child-rearing will be shared. Time spent with the infant will be likely to be calmer and more contented because both parents will have time for other things. Today women transmit the resentment and upset they feel because of the social restrictions in their lives. With two satisfied people to whom to relate the infant's environment will be more likely to be filled with the good food needed for healthy psychological development. Without the push-pull for girls and with both parents tending to and nurturing their daughter, girls will be able to develop a secure sense of self which will enable them to separate psychologically. Boys will not have to separate themselves defensively from mother and create a false sense of secure self in the world whilst repressing an infantile part of themselves. Instead they will be able to incorporate aspects from both mother and father and separate from a position of integration of these aspects into their own psychology.

It will not only be at home that girls and boys will experience both men and women as active in the world as well as nurturant. Children will be at play-schools and nurseries where men and women will be teachers. Men will feel that this is a socially useful and acceptable job for a man. Men will have the ability to relate to children, play and caretake as part of who they have been raised to be.

Because our entire conception of masculine and feminine will be altered, male nursery-school teachers will not have to live with the split in themselves that men today live with of certain activities being feminine and therefore unacceptable for them to do. In all areas of society men and women will be in equal positions, and in a balanced relation to domestic life and productive work away from home.

Several generations from now the variety of family forms that are now emerging will be much more accepted by society. Although we've described a modified heterosexual nuclear family, we do not see it as essential to retain this kind of arrangement to change the balance of emotional labour and hence the addressing of children's and adults' dependency needs. We are restricted in our vision by the society we live in now but new familial arrangements will emerge which will open up new horizons. There may be several couples with children living together and sharing domestic life and child-rearing. There may be lesbian couples raising children together in family units or communally. There may be homosexual men having families together. The psychologies of children growing up in these different environments will be diverse, of course, just as the psychologies of children today growing up with a single parent, or aunts and uncles or grandmothers nearby, or divorced parents, or a parent who dies, differ from the psychology of a child growing up in a traditional nuclear family with father, mother and siblings. The most powerful influence on any child growing up is the ideology of the society. The norm in any society affects children in every aspect of their lives outside the home, even when their home life looks radically different from the norm. In our future projection, even if both sexes are not present in a particular household, children's models will change. Men will be in nurturing roles in other households, in nursery schools and the like. Women will be seen in the home and in the outside world. The multi-dimensional lives of women and men will be visible to all and provide models for children to identify with. If, in generations to come, men and women raise children and boys learn to be nurturers and girls develop as autonomous people out in the world, then whatever the actual form of family life — be it communal, lesbian, heterosexual, homosexual, single parent — all children's psychological development will be radically different from what it is today. Women and men will come to have a different sense of themselves and of each other.

If women and men raise children then our dependency needs will be formed and addressed in different ways. If women can continue to expect their emotional dependency needs to be met then they will no longer feel unworthy of love and undeserving of attention. They will no longer feel insecure in the ways they do today and they will not feel themselves to be clingy people who grasp desperately on to their relationships with men and never feel they are getting what they need.

Independence will no longer be a word used to describe an emotional state of affairs. People will no longer feel that dependency signifies weakness. Dependency will be a normal, healthy part of human life. People will no longer strive to be independent of one another — to stand on their own two feet — to be individualistic and competitive. People's needs for each other, the need for contact and involvement and emotional sharing and care and love, will be accepted as natural to human life. There will be a clearer understanding of the difference between psychological separateness — a complete and secure sense of self — and independence. It will be common knowledge that it is only through satisfaction of our dependency needs and the security of loving and nurturing relationships which provide us with an emotional anchor that we can truly feel autonomous.

Women will no longer carry the dependency in relationships. Women and men will be interdependent and each will have the ability to give nurturance and the ability to receive love and care.

Women and men will no longer look to a partner to fill

empty parts of themselves but instead will approach one another with the desire to be close to another person; to share with one another; to experience pleasure together; to stand by one another in times of stress and pain; to offer one another support and encouragement in developing, creating, and participating fully in life.

These speculations and the future projections may seem far-fetched and hard to achieve but experiments in living arrangements and child-rearing that are going on today already open up interesting possibilities for the next generation of children and adults. Women choosing to raise children on their own or with other women are already beginning to convey a sense of confidence about such arrangements. The word 'family' is taking on a different and broader meaning. The families that today's children live in, and the emotional values and psychologies they are developing, are already moving in the direction of our ideal. We are involved in a social revolution, albeit one that is happening slowly. The possibilities that such developments open up should be looked upon optimistically. What we are seeing now is a foretaste of the kinds of changes that we feel are so very urgent if the sexes are going to bridge the great divide and create a truly equal public and private world together.

Bibliography

Arcana, Judith, *Our Mothers' Daughters*, Women's Press, 1981.

Badinter, Elisabeth, *The Myth of Motherhood*, Souvenir, 1982.

Belotti, Elena Gianini, *Little Girls*, Writers' and Readers' Publishing Co-op, 1975.

Bernard, Jessie, *The Future of Parenthood: The New Role of Mothers*, M. Boyars, 1975.

Bowlby, John, *Attachment and Loss*, Vols. 1 and 2, Hogarth Press, 1969 and 1980.

de Beauvoir, Simone, *The Second Sex*, Cape, 1968; Penguin, 1972.

Deutsch, Helene, *The Psychology of Women*, Vols. 1 and 2, Grune & S., 1944 and 1945.

Dinnerstein, Dorothy, *The Rocking of the Cradle and the Ruling of the World*, Souvenir, 1978.

Dowling, Colette, *The Cinderella Complex*, Michael Joseph, 1982.

Eichenbaum, Luise, and Orbach, Susie, *Outside In ... Inside Out. Women's Psychology: A Feminist Psychoanalytic Approach*, Penguin, 1982.

Foucault, Michel, *The History of Sexuality. Vol. 1: An Introduction*, Allen Lane, 1979.

Friday, Nancy, *My Mother, Myself*, Fontana, 1979.

Guntrip, Harry, *Schizoid Phenomena and Object Relations Theory*, Hogarth Press, 1968.

Hammer, Signe, *Daughters and Mothers, Mothers and Daughters*, Hutchinson, 1976.

Hite, Shere, *The Hite Report*, Corgi, 1981.

Hite, Shere, *The Hite Report on Male Sexuality*, Macdonald, 1981.

Mahler, Margaret S., Pine, Fred, and Bergman, Anni, *The Psychological Birth of the Human Infant: Symbiosis and Individuation*, Hutchinson, 1975.

Orbach, Susie, *Fat is a Feminist Issue*, Hamlyn, 1979. *Fat is a Feminist Issue II*, Hamlyn, 1982.

Scarfe, Maggie, *Unfinished Business*, Fontana, 1981.
Stoller, Robert J., *Sex and Gender: On the Development of Masculinity and Femininity*, Hogarth Press, 1975.
Winnicott, D.W., *The Maturational Processes and the Facilitating Environment*, Hogarth Press, 1965.
Zilbergeld, Bernard, *Men and Sex*, Souvenir, 1979; Fontana, 1980.